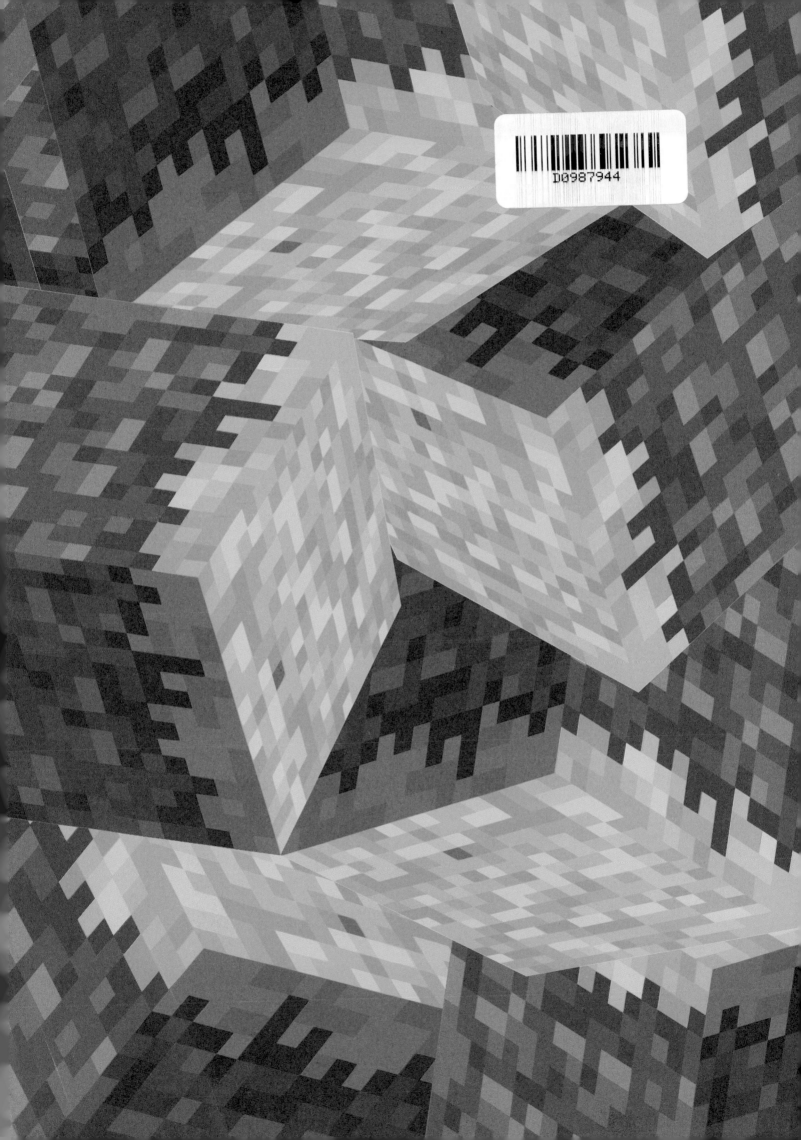

GAMES MASTER

PRESENTS

MINECRAFT

POCKET / PC / MAC / PS4 / XBOX ONE / Wii U / SWITCH / PS3 / 360

PAGE
16
The Ultimate Minecraft Quiz

Test your blocky brains – how many can you get right out of the 50 questions?

PUZZLES

33 CUT OUT AND KEEP MINECRAFT CARDS

PAGE 64

Chicken

Minecart

Mushroom

Bow

GRASSY areas find Chickens, anywhere there space above. Chick in Minecraft to lay to bake Cakes

ATTACK a M eventually y adding it to though, if you a Bow you will de loads of fun!

GRAB an emp Mooshroom to get a Bow Mushroom Stew 6 Hunger points has an 8.5% chance of quite delicious!

THERE are various ways you can get yourself a Bow You can Craft one using 3 Sticks and 3 Strings, you can catch one while Fishing, you can Trade one with a Villager or a Skele has an 8.5% chance of

COVERING MOBS, ITEMS, WEAPONS, VEHICLES, FOOD, ARMOUR & MORE!

PAGE 88
A-Z OF MINECRAFT TIPS

Inside...

KNOW YOUR BIOMES
#1 PLAINS

THE FRIENDLY MOBS JUST LOVE IT AROUND THE PLAINS, AS YOU CAN SEE BY OUR CHICKEN INFESTATION HERE! IT'S ALSO THE ONLY PLACE THAT HORSES WILL SPAWN NATURALLY IN THE GAME.

EXPLORE AND YOU CAN FIND THE ENTRANCE TO CAVES HIDDEN AWAY IN THE TALL GRASS. THE FLAT LANDSCAPE ALSO MAKES IT EASIER TO SPOT LAVA SPRINGS.

WITH BRIGHT GREEN grass blocks and brown dirt, the Plains have the classic look of Minecraft that is instantly recognisable to fans and noobs alike. The Plains are quite a flat area with just a few small hills. You can find pools of water dotted around and passive mobs love spawning here. It's the only place you will find horses spawning naturally.

THE VILLAGERS IN MINECRAFT ALSO LOVE IT ON THE PLAINS. YOU WILL OFTEN FIND VILLAGES APPEAR HERE FOR YOU TO CHECK OUT – MAYBE TRY TRADING WITH THE LOCALS?

THE PLAINS ARE PACKED WITH EVERYTHING YOU NEED TO SURVIVE – CHICKENS, COWS, SHEEP AND PIGS FOR MEAT. WHEAT SEEDS FOR BAKING AND FLOWERS FOR DYES. IT'S A GREAT PLACE TO BUILD YOURSELF A FARM!

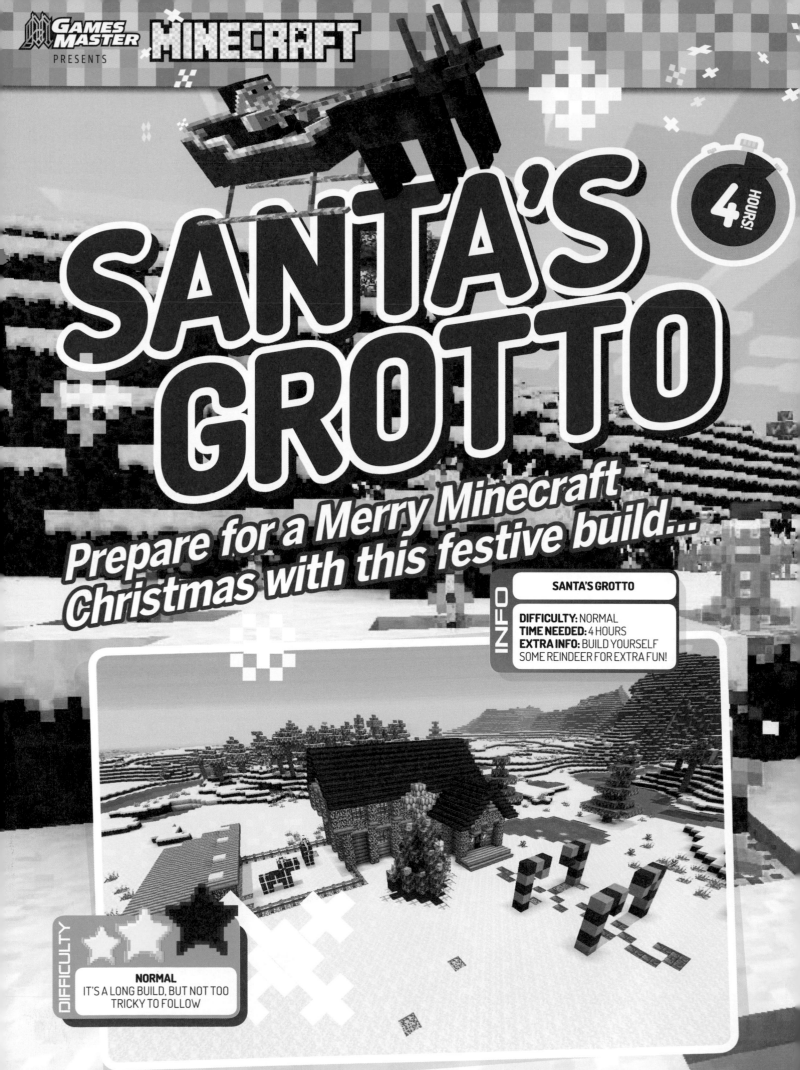

4 HOURS!

SANTA'S GROTTO

Prepare for a Merry Minecraft Christmas with this festive build...

SANTA'S GROTTO

INFO

DIFFICULTY: NORMAL
TIME NEEDED: 4 HOURS
EXTRA INFO: BUILD YOURSELF SOME REINDEER FOR EXTRA FUN!

DIFFICULTY

★★☆

NORMAL
IT'S A LONG BUILD, BUT NOT TOO TRICKY TO FOLLOW

1

SNOW DAY

FIND YOURSELF a frosty **biome** and lay down a Spruce Wood plank floor in an **L-shape**. It's 8x17 with the front bit being 5x6. Place Spruce Wood around the edge with a 2 block gap **in between**.

2

FIRST FLOOR

BUILD IT all 4 blocks high on **top** of your floor layer. Make room for 2x2 windows where you have gaps between the Spruce Wood **pillars**. Place **more Spruce Wood** to build up your pillars.

3

GOING UP

PLACE SLABS to act as your **second** floor. Put some upside-down stairs above your **windows**, so your second floor sticks out a bit. Place Spruce Wood on top all the way around.

4

SMALL ROOF

THE SMALLER bit of your **L-shape** is just your entrance way and won't get a proper floor, so use Dark Oak Plank **stairs** to make a roof on that bit. Make it stick out at the front by 1 **block**.

INSPIRATION

IN ARENDSOOGG'S Christmas Town, Santa even pays a visit! Yo, ho, ho!

SANTA'S CHRISTMAS workshop seems set up for business. Nice one EdiBoy21!

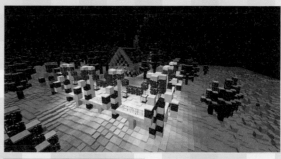

CHRISTMAS VILLAGE by Huskii looks like it's made from gingerbread and candy!

5

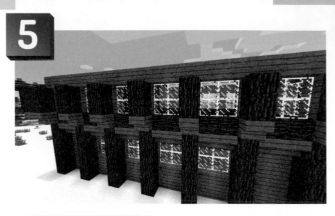

SECOND FLOOR

PUT UPSIDE-down **Stairs** on all of your pillars, then place Spruce Wood going up again to extend them for the **second** floor. Put 2x2 **windows** in the gaps like on the first floor and build your walls up.

6

BIG ROOF

USE DARK Oak Stairs going up to a peak in the middle with Slabs for the very top. Start at the **layer** just above the **windows**. Fill in the gaps where the **small roof joins** to the big one.

7

OPEN ENDS

IT'S TIME to fill in the empty space. Put **upside-down Stairs** above the windows, and **normal Stairs** at the top of your pillars. Add in another 2x2 window and **fill in the rest** with Spruce Planks.

8

FINAL TOUCHES

THE MAIN building just needs a few small final touches. Try adding a porch your front **door** area, and maybe a Stone chimney to the side of the main building. Make sure all of your **pillars are neat**.

9

CANDY CANE LANE

CREATE A path leading up to your **Grotto** with Stone brick blocks hidden **underneath** the Snow. Build **candy** canes made out of White and Red Clay. They're 5 tall, then 2 across and 1 down.

10

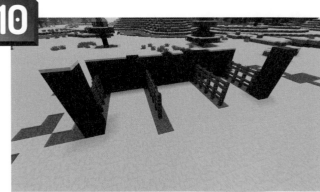

REINDEER STABLES

NOW FOR your **Reindeer** house! Make a 3 high **wall** of Spruce for the back. Then **leave** a gap of 4 blocks and place two pillars of 4 high at each end. Place Spruce Fence walls 2 blocks high to make pens.

11

SLANTED ROOF

TO MAKE the **slope of the roof**, use thin Slabs on top of the back **wall** and one block behind. Go up 1 space for the next 2 rows, and then 1 space again for the last 2. Put **gates** on your fence pens.

12

LIVESTOCK

NOW WE just need some **Reindeer** to live in the pens! First create a fenced area that connects to the **Grotto** for them to live in. Then build your **deer** out of Brown Wool, Steel Fence and Buttons.

INSPIRATION

STARGO123 put together this snowy Christmas Surprise just in time for Santa!

CHRISTMAS VALLEY from Team Surface looks like the most festive place on earth!

LOOK AT all the nice presents to unwrap in Chomp2's holiday homestead!

13

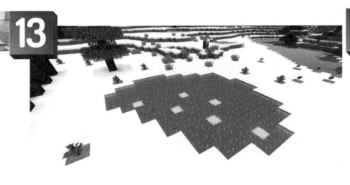

ICE AS NICE

WHAT DOES Santa do when he wants to relax? He skates! Build an ice rink to the right of the **Grotto** by digging a 1 block deep hole and placing Ice over the top. Put Sea **Lanterns** underneath to light it.

14

IT'S CHRISTMAS!

PUT A Christmas Tree at the front of the **Grotto**. Use carpet as a mat in an almost round shape with a **Spruce** Wood trunk in the middle and build up. Decorate with Wool, and a Glowstone star on top.

YOU WILL NEED: Sticky Pistons, Redstone Torches, Redstone Dust, Redstone Repeaters, Redstone Block, Lever, Stone Brick Blocks (or choose any other type you like), Lava, Dirt

MASTER REDSTONE!

How to make a draw bridge rise up and down from lava using Redstone!

1 BLOCK PATH

Dig a hole 4 blocks deep and 6 blocks wide. This bridge will be 2 blocks wide, so you want to make 2 rows of Stone Brick blocks with a 2 block gap in-between and then put Redstone Dust along the top of them.

HOW TO MAKE ME BOIL IN FIERY ROCK JUICE!

2 LIGHT IT UP

Put Redstone Torches on the side of every block, and then put a Sticky Piston directly above each one. Since the Torches are on, they'll shoot right up. Put blocks on top – you want this layer to line up with your path on either side.

3 CIRCUIT PATH

Connect the Redstone Dust together at one end then place a Lever and you'll have a working drawbridge! But we want to use it from *inside* our building. So dig a path under your building to get inside, placing Redstone Dust as you go. Put down a Repeater every few blocks facing towards your bridge to keep the signal strong.

THAT MOAT LOOKS LIKE A RIVER OF BAKED BEANS!

4 SIGNAL LEVER

Now the circuit is inside we need to get it up to ground height. To do this we're going to place a Lever on a block and then send a signal *down* to our Redstone Circuit. Place a Sticky Piston underneath your lever block with a Redstone block beneath that. The lever will make the block go up and down.

5 MIND THE GAP

Make sure that when the Piston is fully out with the Redstone block there's a 1 block space underneath it – if it touches the ground it will crush the Redstone Dust underneath and only work once. Use Redstone Dust to connect the block underneath to your circuit, and woof! Your drawbridge should now go up and down.

6 COVER UP

Now time to hide all the Redstone so you can pour in your Lava moat. Make sure you place Dirt 1 block above all of the Redstone so you don't accidentally break it, and make sure there aren't any gaps where Lava could get in. Fill in all of your Lava over the top and you'll have finished your deadly bridge!

GUESS THE MOB

Can you tell these mobs from their shadows?

1

I'm...

....

2

I'm...

....

3

I'm...

....

4

I'm...

....

5

I'm...

....

ANSWERS
ON PAGE
93

QUICK BUILD!

Fill your skies with hot air balloons. Up, up and away!

5 MINUTES!

START HERE!

1 BUILD a basket with Wood plants in a 3x3 square base, Wood at the corners and upside down Stairs at the edges.

2 PLACE Wood Posts 4 blocks high, then fill the area inside their tops with Wool. Step up and out from this 2 times.

3 NOW go straight up 2 blocks to make the large flat faces, then back and up a block twice to make the top bit. Fill it in.

4 ADD detail by giving the balloon a coloured stripe and adding a burner to the bottom using a Glowstone.

BUILD THIS!

DIFFICULTY

EASY
YOU WILL SOON BE READY FOR TAKE OFF IN THIS BALLOON!

THE ULTIMATE MINECRAFT QUIZ!

Think you know about Minecraft? Well it's time to prove yourself – test your brains with our 50 tricky questions on the world's greatest game!

TICK THE ANSWER THAT YOU THINK IS RIGHT – WHEN YOU'RE DONE, CHECK IF YOU'RE RIGHT ON PAGE 93!

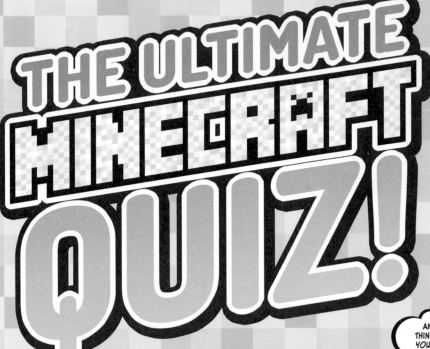

1 What is the minimum amount of blocks needed to make a Nether Portal?

A. 10

B. 8

C. 12

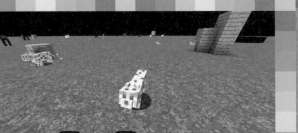

2 Which biome do Ocelots spawn in?

A. Desert

B. Jungle

C. Hills

3 How long is a day in Minecraft?

A. 24 hours

B. 1 hour

C. 20 minutes

4 What potion effect do you get when you use a Rabbit's Foot in brewing?

A. Leaping

B. Speed

C. Regeneration

5 If a Villager gets struck by lightning, what happens to them?
A. They burn
B. They turn into a potato
C. They turn into a witch

6 Name the man who created Minecraft and sold it for $3.5 billion!
A. Bennett
B. Lucas
C. Notch

7 Which of these are multiplayer games in console Minecraft...
A. Tumble
B. Clash
C. Glide

8 How do you craft a bed?
A. 3 Wool and 3 Wood Planks
B. A duvet and some pillows
C. 3 Wool and 2 Sticks

9 Which is the rarest Ore?
A. Redstone
B. Diamond
C. Emerald

10 What happens when a scary Creeper gets struck by lightning?
A. It turns into a charged Creeper with larger blast radius
B. It freezes where it's stood
C. It asks you to a tea party

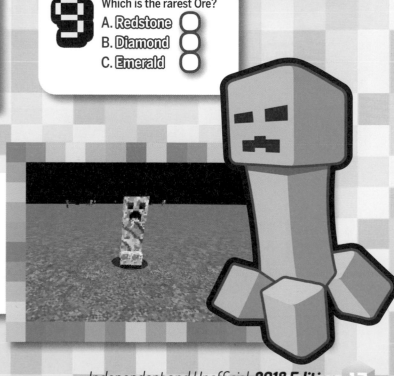

11 What type of tools run out the quickest?
A. Wooden tools
B. Golden tools
C. Iron tools

12 Name the dragon found in The End.
A. The Ender Dragon
B. The Nether Dragon
C. Smaug

13 What happens if you eat Chorus fruit found in The End?
A. You swell to twice the size
B. You are teleported to a location within 8 blocks
C. You turn into a cow

14 What is the name of the story game created by Telltale Games?
A. Tell us a Story
B. Minecraft: Story Mode
C. Minecraft the Tale

15 Which items do you need to craft a Cake?
A. 1 Egg, 2 Cocoa Beans, 2 Wheat
B. 1 Egg, 2 Wheat, 4 Milk Buckets
C. 1 Egg, 2 Sugar, 3 Wheat, 3 Milk Buckets

16 Which substance acts as electricity in Minecraft?
A. Wirestone
B. Rougestone
C. Redstone

17 How do you get saddles?
A. You craft them
B. They are found in spawned buildings
C. You find them on Pigs

18 Which country was Minecraft originally made in?
A. England
B. Sweden
C. America

19 How many different kinds of biomes are there in PC Minecraft? (Two are unused!)
A. 63
B. 53
C. 43

20 What do pigs eat?
A. Sandwiches
B. Seeds
C. Carrots

MINECRAFT

 21 What do you use to mine Stone with?

A. Sword
B. Pickaxe
C. Drill

22 Which of these items do Zombies NOT drop...

A. Iron Ingots
B. Potatoes
C. Candy Floss

23 Which of these blocks cannot be pushed by a Piston?

A. Melon Block
B. Stone Block
C. Wool Block

24 How many types of tree are there in Minecraft?

A. 5
B. 8
C. 6

25 What kind of Ore is found in The Nether?

A. Strawberry
B. Coal
C. Nether Quartz

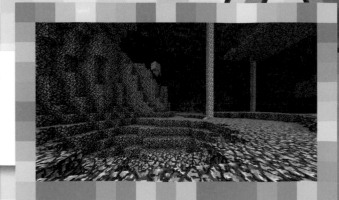

27 How many colours of Wool are there?
A. 16
B. 18
C. 22

26 Which of these is NOT a Minecraft mob?
A. Ghast
B. Crocodile
C. Polar bear

28 What do Squid drop when killed?
A. Steak
B. Ink Sacs
C. Melons

29 How many hearts of damage does an ordinary Diamond Sword deal?
A. 5 Hearts
B. 7 Hearts
C. 9 Hearts

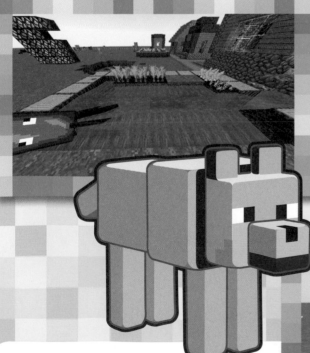

30 How do you tame Wolves?
A. Give them a bone
B. Put them on a lead
C. Feed them some steak

THE QUIZ CONTINUES ON PAGE... **48**

KNOW YOUR BIOMES
#2 MUSHROOM ISLAND

THE LANDSCAPE ON A MUSHROOM ISLAND IS FAIRLY FLAT FOR THE MOST PART, WITH STEEP HILLS POPPING UP. THE MUSHROOMS GIVE IT A RED WITH WHITE SPOTS LOOK.

THE ONLY MOB THAT SPAWNS ON A MUSHROOM ISLAND IS THE MOOSHROOM. NO OTHER MOB CAN NATURALLY SPAWN HERE, BUT THEY CAN APPEAR THROUGH MOB SPAWNERS.

FOUND ALL ON their own, isolated from other biomes, the Mushroom Island is a rare place indeed! It doesn't have any Grass, instead having Mycelium blocks covering the ground, and water all around. Giant mushrooms grow here as they can get lots of sunshine and you won't find any hostile mobs here, so feel free to explore and mine in peace!

TRY MILKING THE MOOSHROOMS FOUND ON A MUSHROOM ISLAND. YOU WILL GET A DELICIOUS MUSHROOM STEW, AND THEY WILL TURN BACK INTO REGULAR OLD COWS!

BEING SURROUNDED BY OCEAN, MUSHROOM ISLANDS ARE A SAFE PLACE TO TAKE SHELTER. EVEN AT NIGHT YOU CAN WANDER AROUND IN SAFETY.

MAKE YOUR OWN STORY

PUT YOURSELF into the heart of a new Minecraft story. All you need to do is take a pen or pencil and fill in the blanks in the story below with your own name, and your ideas of what would make the story really epic!

Title: _____

One day, the new Minecraft hero _____ had just spawned into a brand new world. There was a sign saying, "This world is called _____ and belongs to _____."

"Wow, said _____, how exciting. I wonder what kind of mobs live in a place like this?" The hero first set about building a house, to protect from the night-time mobs. They used _____ blocks and put _____ inside a chest. Then _____ set off to explore this new world.

Turning the corner in a village, _____ came across a super-scary _____ mob. It was coloured _____ and had great big _____ coming out of its head! "_____!" shouted _____ and started to run away.

Just then, a giant _____ mob appeared from behind the clouds. It smelled of _____ and was all scaly with giant outstretched wings. It landed on the Grass blocks just in front of our hero and hissed, "_____!" _____ climbed on the back of this beast and they took off.

The view from up in the air on the back of the _____ was breathtaking! "I can see my house from up here!" shouted _____. The beast thought our hero said, "You can land on my house," and swooped down, sitting on the roof with a thud. CRASH! All that was left was a big pile of _____ blocks.

PUZZLES

Test your brains with these teasers...

HAVE YOU GOT BRAINS? I'M REALLY HUNGRY!

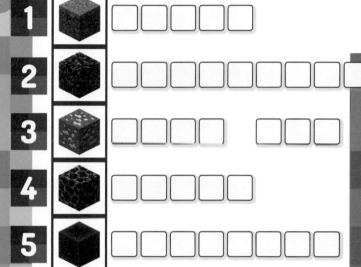

WEAPON SUDOKU

CAN YOU fill in the blank squares with weapons, making sure that each row of 4 has only one of each? Oh, and each block of 4 also has to have only one of each. Draw in the missing weapons and we'll see how much of a brain box you are!

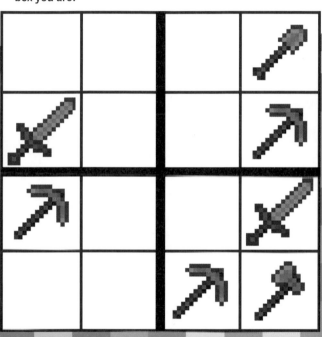

NAME THAT BLOCK

WHAT WOULD a game of Minecraft be without blocks? They come in all shapes, sizes, colours (and smells?). How well do you think you know your Iron Ore from your Coal? Now is the time to shine...

1
2
3
4
5
6
7

HAVE YOU GOT THEM ALL RIGHT? THE ANSWERS ARE ON PAGE 93

HOW MANY SPIDERS?

WOAH LOOK OUT! Our world has been overrun by deadly spiders. Maybe it's our deodorant attracting them? While we find a sword to sort them out, can you count how many there are? Can you spot the bonus rabbit?

ANSWERS ON PAGE 93

WRITE IN HOW MANY YOU FOUND!

KNOW YOUR BIOMES
#3 FOREST

THE FOREST BIOME IS A GREAT PLACE TO START OUT ON YOUR MINECRAFT ADVENTURE AS IT HAS LOTS OF WOOD FOR YOU TO CHOP DOWN – PERFECT FOR MAKING YOUR FIRST MINECRAFT HOUSE!

WE DON'T RECOMMEND EXPLORING THE FOREST BIOME AT NIGHT – IT CAN BE A VERY DANGEROUS PLACE AS THE TREES CAN HIDE ALL KINDS OF NASTY MOBS!

IF THERE ARE a lot of Birch and Oak trees around, then you're in a Forest biome. There will be a lot of tall Grass all around, and there will likely be hills dotted about the landscape. You can find Flowers and Mushrooms if you forage in the undergrowth. Obviously, a Forest biome is a great place for stocking up on different kinds of Wood.

WITH SO MUCH WOOD, YOU WILL SOON BE MAKING A CRAFTING TABLE WHICH WILL START YOUR GAME OFF WELL!

AS YOU CAN SEE, WE HAD A BUNCH OF COWS FOLLOW US TO THE FOREST BIOME, BUT ONE OF THE ANIMALS YOU WILL FIND IN ABUNDANCE IS THE WOLF!

Make it!
GRASS BLOCK CRISPIES!

The first block we all remember – the grass block. Now in crispy cake form!

INFO

GRASS BLOCK CRISPIES

TIME NEEDED: 60 MINUTES
EXTRA INFO: OR MAKE IT SUPER-EASY AND CHOP UP SOME RICE CRISPIES SQUARES!

YOU'LL NEED...

INGREDIENTS: 60g butter, 280g marshmallows, 340g chocolate, 250g puffed rice cereal, 200g icing sugar, drop of green colouring
PREPARATION: Wash your hands!

1 WEIGHING & PREP

WOW! CAN you imagine eating a Minecraft Grass Block for your tea? Well, we are here to make your Willy Wonka-style dreams come true! We have given weights and measurements in the ingredients above, but you will need to ask a grown up to help you adjust these based on the size of the bowl you have, the amount of rice cereal and chocolate you have, and how many Crafters you want to feed! First, take a bit of the butter and spread it all around your square(ish) dish that will form the Grass Block cube shapes.

BE SURE TO GET THE BUTTER INTO ALL THE CORNERS – OR IT WILL STICK!

WARNING

ASK MUM, DAD, OR WHOEVER LOOKS AFTER YOU TO HELP WITH HEATING IN A MICROWAVE

YOU DON'T HAVE TO BE EXACT IN YOUR WEIGHING

2 I'M MELTING!

WEIGH OUT the butter, marshmallows and chocolate then break it all up into as many small pieces as you can. If you use chocolate chips, you won't need to do this, but we used chocolate bars. Put all these small pieces into a big mixing bowl and microwave it for one minute. Take out the bowl, give it a stir with a wooden spoon, then pop it back in for another minute. Careful as the marshmallows will expand before they go gooey. Repeat this, mixing it up each time, until you have brown goo! It should take between 3-4 minutes.

3 MAKING DIRT

WITH YOUR big bowl of brown goo still warm, add the puffed rice cereal and slowly mix the rice in to the goo. Take it carefully at this stage as it can get very messy, and the marshmallow and chocolate goo sticks to any spoon, knife or finger you put in it! We found two regular knives worked best – you can use them to scrape the mixture off each other as you mix the rice into the goo.

CAREFULLY FOLD IN THE RICE CEREAL

4 SQUARING IT UP

WITH THE ingredients nicely mixed up, you're now ready to gloop it into your prepared dish. Square dishes give you a head start in making your blocks, but the important thing is to press the mixture down hard to form a solid block. Once you've pressed it all around and it starts to cool, you will find you can fold it back on itself to make blocks as high as you want. Press from the sides and above to make a solid and square cake!

YOU WANT YOUR BLOCKS TO BE BLOCK SHAPED, SO IF YOUR DISH IS TOO DEEP, FOLD THE MIXTURE BACK ON ITSELF

5 CHILL, MAN!

NOW IT'S time to chill your creation in the fridge. Give it about an hour to let everything get nice and solid. While it's doing this you can measure out your icing ingredients. Put the icing sugar into a bowl with a knob of butter and add 1 desert spoon of hot water at a time to make a thick icing (ask a grown up to help with hot things!), give this a good mix. Now add a couple of drops of green food colouring and mix like crazy again to get green icing! Once your dirt cake has got cool and hard, spread the green icing over the top and use a fork to tease the icing up to make grass!

TRY ADDING DRIED CRANBERRIES TO MAKE A REDSTONE CRISPY BLOCK!

LET YOUR CAKE WARM UP TO ROOM TEMPERATURE BEFORE YOU CHOP IT IF IT'S STUCK

YOU CAN TEASE THE TOP OF THE ICING WITH A FORK TO MAKE IT LOOK LIKE GRASS!

FINISHED!

GIVE YOUR giant Grass Block Crispy Cake another hour in the fridge, then you can chop it up into cube shapes ready for your Minecraft party! Ask a grown up to help again here as you will need a sharp knife and some muscle as the Grass Block Crispies will be hard! Now just munch away and enjoy!

Vloggers!

Need some helpful advice or fun projects to enjoy? Here are the latest and greatest videos from our hand-picked YouTubers. Let's press play...

STAMPYLONGHEAD

REAL NAME:
JOSEPH GARRETT
FROM: ENGLAND
SUBSCRIBERS: 8,356,875
VIEWS: 5,855,377,932
FUN FACT: HE HAS TWO BOOKS OUT NOW!
MOST VIEWED VIDEO: "MINECRAFT XBOX – SINKING FEELING" – 51,787,292 VIEWS

BOUNCING BOATS

Stampy is building a slippy, slidey boat game using Ice blocks in the Xbox 360 version. He has a giant Fun Land that he has been working on! Along with his team of builders, he shows you how to get the boat ride working using Slime Launchers, Obsidian, Redstone and two Pistons, eagerly watched by his dog, Barnaby. When he opens up his theme park, will you be queuing to get in? We'll see you there!

SINKING FEELING

The most watched Stampy video of all time! It's getting close to being watched 52 million times. Stampy's theme park is coming on nicely, and in this video he's building a Raindrop game where you fall out of the clouds and land on a raindrop. Sounds dangerous! He is building incredibly high in the air. We're sure we could see our house from up there! There are always lots of great tips to be had from Stampy.

DAN TDM

REAL NAME:
DAN MIDDLETON
FROM: ENGLAND
SUBSCRIBERS: 14,511,419
VIEWS: 9,516,658,734
FUN FACT: TDM ACTUALLY MEANS 'THE DIAMOND MINECART'. BUT YOU KNEW THAT, RIGHT?
MOST VIEWED VIDEO: "BEST OF DIAMOND MINECART" – 38,721,369 VIEWS

PIXELMON TRINITY #3

Dan enjoys playing the Pixelmon mod in Minecraft. He knows this Pokémon mod inside out, installing a great looking mini-map. He's out to capture Pokémon, but needs to buy a Poké Ball first selling the Apricorns he's been collecting. He's got a brilliant Monferno in his team and gets to battle with Team Rocket. If you want to pick up more Pixelmon tips, this is a great video to watch.

BEST OF DIAMOND MINECART

Dan has been creating his Minecraft videos for five years, and there have been lots of great moments! The most popular video on his channel is the 'Best of Diamond Minecart' compilation including a very weird bit where he gets squished by a bunch of naked people! He has actually won a Guinness World Record for the 'Most views for any dedicated Minecraft video channel' – well done Dan!

SOME OF THESE VIDEOS HAVE BEEN WATCHED OVER A MILLION TIMES!

ERR... IS THAT MORE THAN 5?

YouTube: Vloggers

WARNING

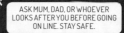

ASK MUM, DAD, OR WHOEVER LOOKS AFTER YOU BEFORE GOING ON LINE. STAY SAFE.

POPULAR MMOS

REAL NAMES: PATRICK JULIANELLE & JENNIFER FLAGG

FROM: FLORIDA, USA

SUBSCRIBERS: 11,055,101

VIEWS: 7,968,733,010

FUN FACT: THESE TWO YOUTUBERS ARE MARRIED!

MOST VIEWED VIDEO: "MORE TNT MOD (35 TNT EXPLOSIVES AND DYNAMITE!)" – 36,734,645 VIEWS

YOU WOULD NEVER EXPECT THIS!!!

Married couple Pat and Jen have posted a collection of funny moments in Minecraft for you to enjoy. Even though they make many of the maps themselves, they often forget what they've built and give themselves jump scares! They certainly enjoy making vids – they can't stop laughing! Jen also has her own YouTube channel called GamingWithJen.

TOO MUCH TNT MOD

Learn everything Pat knows about the various TNT Blocks in the 'Too Much TNT' mod in this video that has been watched nearly a whopping 37 million times. Have you seen what Meteor TNT can do to a world?! Woah – the explosion left a giant hole! Compact TNT is a tiny block that when it explodes turns into regular TNT blocks. So much explosive action in one video – everyone loves blowing stuff up!

SKY DOES MINECRAFT

REAL NAME: ADAM DAHLBERG

FROM: WASHINGTON, USA

SUBSCRIBERS: 12,014,352

VIEWS: 3,466,041,490

FUN FACT: HE WAS ONCE PART OF THE MINECRAFT GROUP TEAM CRAFTED!

MOST VIEWED VIDEO: "NEW WORLD - A MINECRAFT PARODY OF COLDPLAY'S PARADISE" – 76,209,706 VIEWS

THE SQUID RETURNS

Sky Does Minecraft does regular Let's Play Minecraft videos, but in between these you'll find brilliant story vids (they're called Machinima, if you didn't know. It's making stories in games). In his latest instalment, we see that a Squid has been kept captive for years and tries to persuade Sky Does Minecraft to let him free. "One of these days I will get my revenge on you Sky," says Squid. Well we'll see about that!

NEW WORLD

We love this! Sky Does Minecraft sings the lead vocals in a jokey version of Coldplay's Paradise music video. If you've not seen this yet (surely you're one of the 76 million viewers?) then you must! The animation is really professional (it's made by Slamacow) and it's packed with great jokes and Minecraft fun. We particularly love the white Creeper drum kit that they are playing – we want one! Great stuff.

Vloggers!

WHAT DO CAVEMEN SLEEP ON AT NIGHT?

CAPTAIN SPARKLEZ

REAL NAME:
JORDAN MARON

FROM: USA

SUBSCRIBERS: 9,870,169

VIEWS: 2,790,161,115

FUN FACT: HE HAS A HOUSE IN THE HOLLYWOOD HILLS

MOST VIEWED VIDEO: "REVENGE" – A MINECRAFT ORIGINAL MUSIC VIDEO – 167,397,228 VIEWS

ST JOSEPHINE'S HORROR HOSPITAL W/X33N

Do you like a good jump scare? Who doesn't, right? This video from Captain Sparkles is packed with them as he explores the spooky St Josephine's Hospital with fellow Crafter X33N. This is not a map for scaredy cats, it's full of what these two call "strawberry jam incidents" as they wander the old hospital corridors.

REVENGE – MUSIC VIDEO

It is time to get funky! This is one mightly popular Minecraft music video with over 167 million views and counting. Captain Sparkles has done the animation and written some of the lyrics, but he's joined by TryHardNinja on lead vocals. With lines like, "Cause baby tonight, the creeper's trying to steal your stuff again, again, again" you're going to be humming this tune in the playground once you've heard it!

BAJAN CANADIAN

REAL NAME:
MITCHELL HUGHES

FROM: FLORIDA, USA

SUBSCRIBERS: 5,938,553

VIEWS: 1,731,498,178

FUN FACT: HE HAS HIS OWN BOOK OUT CALLED 'REALITY RESPAWNS'

MOST VIEWED VIDEO: "HUNGER GAMES SONG" – A MINECRAFT PARODY OF DECISIONS BY BORGORE – 88,623,542 VIEWS

2 TEAMERS VS 1 PRO?!

Mitch is playing Bed Wars, but doesn't seem to be too good at this multiplayer game and keeps falling off the map! He's the pro and he takes on two other players, while his commentary will give you a bunch of hints and tips on improving your own game. Bajan Canadian's videos don't seem to get the viewers they used to, and many fans are discussing why in the comments, but we still love watching him!

HUNGER GAMES SONG

This one dates back to 2013 and is all about the Hunger Games mini-game that Bajan Canadian created. The song has vocals by Jake and John and is based on a song by Borgore, who gave his blessing to this Minecraft version being made! With animation by AtomicMonkeyPro, you have to wonder what Bajan Canadian did? Well he brought it to his nearly six million subscribers we guess!

BEDROCK OF COURSE!

PAUL SOARES JR

WARNING

ASK MUM, DAD, OR WHOEVER LOOKS AFTER YOU BEFORE GOING ON LINE. STAY SAFE.

REAL NAME:
NO, IT IS REALLY PAUL SOARES JR.

FROM: BOSTON, USA

SUBSCRIBERS: 1,471,612

VIEWS: 486,682,037

FUN FACT: PAUL'S WIFE GOES BY THE NAME 'MINECRAFTMOM'

MOST VIEWED VIDEO: "MINECRAFT TUTORIAL 01 (V2) - HOW TO SURVIVE YOUR FIRST NIGHT" – 8,775,475 VIEWS

LEGO WORLDS EPISODE 2

Paul has recently turned his hand to the new LEGO Worlds (it's like Minecraft, only made out of LEGO). In this second episode he blasts off in a spaceship to a prehistoric world packed with gold bricks, LEGO minifigures and some hilarious props. Just like Minecraft, LEGO Worlds can be played in a simple way, but underneath it has an incredible level of complexity, and Paul peels back some of these layers showing you how to customise your avatar.

HOW TO SURVIVE YOUR FIRST NIGHT

If you're a Minecraft Noob then Paul's videos are perfect for you. He was actually one of the first people to ever post tutorial videos on Minecraft and this video dates back to 2010 (were you even born then?)! It's packed with really useful tips on learning the basics of the game from the very first tree chop, and a video that all newbies need to watch a couple of times to get up to speed.

IBALLISTICSQUID

REAL NAME:
DAVID SPENCER

FROM: YORKSHIRE

SUBSCRIBERS: 12,014,352

VIEWS: 3,466,041,490

FUN FACT: YOU CAN OFTEN SEE STAMPY IN IBALLISTICSQUID'S VIDEOS!

MOST VIEWED VIDEO: "SKY ISLAND CHALLENGE - RESCUE MISSION!!" – 15,647,636 VIEWS

FUNNIEST BEDWARS GAME!

Watch as iBallisticSquid plays the Waterfall map in Bed Wars. He gets off to a bit of a bad start and loses his precious bed really quickly, but then he warms up a bit. There are some hilarious moments to be had in this video, and lots of great tips to improve your multiplayer games in Minecraft Bed Wars. You must always be sure to build a fortress around your bed, but have you tried adding water on top to spray at those hacking at it?

SKY ISLAND CHALLENGE – RESCUE MISSION!!

iBallisticSquid rises to the challenge of Stampylongnose's Sky Island back in 2013, that's like a million years ago in YouTube time! It's good to see the team working well together: Stampy, White Fang and Buildaholic as they try to rescue Auntie Squid, the last Squid family member, who has been kidnapped! Will they do it?

5 HOURS!

HAUNTED HOUSE!

Build a creepy home for your friends to visit!

DIFFICULTY

★★★

HARD
THIS IS A BIG BUILD, SO MAKE
SURE YOU FOLLOW CLOSELY

INFO

HAUNTED HOUSE

DIFFICULTY: HARD
TIME NEEDED: 5 HOURS
EXTRA INFO: GO FURTHER AND
MAKE A WHOLE VILLAGE!

1

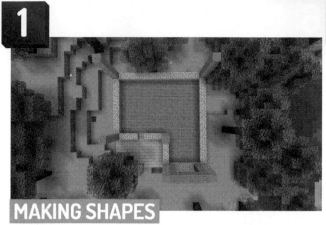

MAKING SHAPES

LAY YOUR foundations and put in a floor so it's all flat to build from. The **whole area is a 15x15 square**, but make your building an **L shape** with some **outside space** to make it more interesting.

2

BUILD YOUR WALLS

YOU WANT the first floor walls to be **5 blocks** high because tall ceilings feel creepier. Use Cobblestone for the **bottom layer** and Planks for the others, with **Tree Trunks** in each of the corners for texture.

3

GOING UP

AFTER ADDING in some windows it's time to build a **second floor**. Use Tree Trunks to show the change in floors, and then use just **Planks** for your walls. We made this layer just **4 blocks** high.

4

STEP UP

ADD IN A STAIRCASE to get to your **upper floor**. Make it twist and **hide it with a wall** so it feels **dark and scary**. Use Redstone Torches for light as they are darker than normal ones.

INSPIRATION

CREEPSHOW Jar9's classic spook house looks like a haunted hotel from the movies!

DEVIL HORNS With its tusks and towers, Dalaxys's house just screams "Run away!"

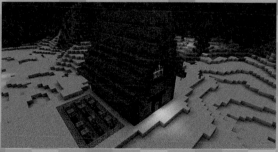

SPOOK SHACK Everyone knows the littlest haunts are the scariest, eh Ender Lord 333!

5

COVER UP

USE STAIRS to make a simple **stepping up roof** with Planks on top. Make sure it sticks out on all sides by 1 block. We tested **Stone** and **Dark Oak**, but chose the **Wood** in the end!

6

COME TOGETHER

START WITH the **roof edges**, including the small bit of your L to make sure it **all lines up** when it joins. The small bit won't be as high as the main roof. Now give your **attic** a few windows.

7

SECRET WALL

NOW IT'S TIME to **decorate**! You can make a **secret path** using a large painting by making a 1x2 block walkway and using Sign Posts to **trick the painting** into thinking it's a solid wall.

8

HOME SWEET HOME

IT'S STILL a house even if it is **haunted**, so adding some chairs and maybe a coffee table will keep it feeling more like a home. **Make it creepy** by adding **Cobwebs** and the **weird clown painting**.

9

DAMP CELLAR

NO HAUNTED HOUSE worth its salt is complete without a **scary basement**, so you'd better dig a **small room** underneath your house. Add some prison cells using **Iron bars** for extra creepiness!

10

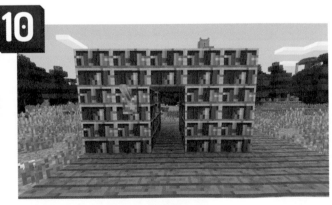

REDSTONE BOOKCASE

IT WOULDN'T be a haunted house without a **secret passage** hidden by a **Bookcase**! We're showing it outside to make it easy to see, but be sure to put yours in a **dark corner** of your house.

INSPIRATION

FOREST FEAR Fancepants proves that a spooky house is spookier with woods!

FRIGHT HOUSE Starferret goes one better and gives us a massive haunted mansion!

TERROR TOWERS This dark and imposing build by GreyHavens gives us the shivers!

11

SOMETHING STICKY

YOU'LL NEED 6 Sticky Pistons – 4 facing out to the side, and then two that face towards where you want your **secret door** to be. Put some Bookshelves in front of the **visible sticky bits**.

12

CIRCUITRY

PLACE WOOL around the top of your **Pistons** to make it easy to **see your circuit**. Put Redstone Dust along the top and a Repeater set to 2 or 3 on top of your **back Piston**. Now test it with a Lever.

13

HIDE AWAY

USE MORE cases for the **sides of your path** and put Redstone Dust along them until it's **behind the front Bookcase**. It's enough to **activate** it so you can put your Lever here. Now cover it all up!

14

SMASH IT UP

THE LAST STEP is to make the place look old and abandoned. **Smash windows**, place Cobwebs, swap Stairs for Planks to make it look like bits of wall are missing. You want **messy** rather than **neat** here!

KNOW YOUR BIOMES
#4 EXTREME HILLS

YOU MUST BE REALLY CAREFUL WHEN EXPLORING EXTREME HILLS IN SURVIVAL MODE – FALLING FROM THESE HEIGHTS IS DEADLY – THERE ARE LOTS OF SHEER CLIFFS AND LEDGES.

DIG DOWN THROUGH THE HILLS AND YOU WILL FIND THE LARGEST NUMBER OF UNDERGROUND CAVERNS IN ANY MINECRAFT BIOME. YOU CAN MINE LOTS OF EMERALD ORE HERE.

WANT TO GET a good view of your creations in Minecraft? Then you need to climb to the mountaintops in the Extreme Hills biome. A mixture of hills, mountains, valleys, caverns, waterfalls and cliffs, you will find just a few scattered Spruce and Oak trees around. As the Extreme Hills can rise to above 130 blocks in height, you can get Snow on the tops of the mountains.

THE MAIN GROUND BLOCK FOUND IN EXTREME HILLS IS GRAVEL. THERE ARE OAK AND SPRUCE TREES DOTTED AROUND FOR WOOD, AND DIG DOWN TO FIND EMERALD ORE. YOU CAN ALSO PICK A FEW FLOWERS WHILE YOU'RE HERE!

THE EXTREME HILLS IS THE ONLY BIOME WHERE THE LLAMA NATURALLY SPAWNS IN MINECRAFT. WATCH OUT THOUGH OR YOU'LL GET SPAT AT! THE OTHER MOB AROUND HERE IS THE SILVERFISH THAT WILL BURST OUT FROM MINED STONES, SO BE ON YOUR GUARD!

MAKE AN ENDERMAN CARD!

DIFFICULTY: EASY
TIME NEEDED: 20 MINS
TELL MUM? YES – YOU MAY NEED HELP WITH SCISSORS

Make it!
MAKE AN ENDERMAN CARD

Surprise unsuspecting friends or family with a pop-up card. Heck, at least this way they're fine to look him in the eye.

YOU'LL NEED...

MATERIALS: 2 sheets of purple card, 1 sheet of black paper, scrap paper, double-sided sticky tape, scissors, ruler, purple and silver sparkly gel pens.

1 PURPLE CARD

First things first: you need to make your basic card that the pop-out will, well, pop out from. Take a piece of purple card that's twice the size you want your finished card to be, and fold it in half. We used a sheet of A4 card for this, but you could go as big or as small as you like. You want the fold to be nice and precise, so go over it a few times with your thumbnail.

2 CUT & FOLD

From your other sheet of purple card, measure and cut out a rectangle 5cm long and 1cm wide (this is assuming you used an A4 piece of card in step 1 – you'll need to make it a bit longer/shorter for a bigger/smaller card). Fold this rectangle in half, and fold each end towards the middle, about 1cm from the edge.

GET AN ADULT TO HELP YOU WITH THE SCISSORS

3 MARK IT UP

Open up your card base, and make two small pen marks – each 3cm from the central fold – roughly in the middle of the card's height. They're only for reference, and will soon be covered up, so make sure you keep them nice and small. This is the guide for your pop-up, so make sure they're even!

MAKE A TINY MARK 3CM FROM THE MIDDLE OF YOUR CARD

4 ADD THE HINGE

The little tabs on your card rectangle will act as feet for your pop-up – the small piece of card will act like a small hinge that stands up when you open the card. Cut two pieces of double-sided sticky tape that are the same size as these feet, and use them to attach your hinge to the card – stick each foot to one of the guide marks you made in step 3. To make sure these stick really well, it's worth closing your card and placing some heavy books on top of it while you carry on with the next couple of steps.

STICK THE HINGE TO THE CARD AT YOUR PEN MARK

6 CUT IT OUT

Once you've got an Enderman template that you're happy with, use it as a guide to carefully cut out your Enderman figure from your black paper. He'll need to have a fold going down his middle, so – as you did with your sketch – it will probably help to fold your black paper in half. Once you've done that, use your gel pens to give him his chilling, characteristic eyes.

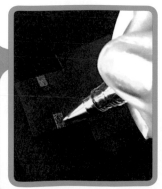

5 MAKE A TEMPLATE

Using some scrap paper, sketch out your Enderman figure, and then cut it out. You don't want him to be any taller or wider than your card – in fact, you want him just to pop out of the middle – so keep that in mind while you're drawing. As he's such a prominent feature of your card, it's also a good idea to fold your scrap paper in half, and sketch out just half of the figure against the fold – that way he'll be perfectly symmetrical when you cut him out. Don't worry if you're not great at drawing – this is just a template, and you can take as many tries as you need!

USING LINED PAPER MIGHT HELP YOU

7 ATTACH THE MAN

Salvage your card from under those books, and open it up. Put a strip of double-sided tape across the back of your Enderman (roughly where his belly button would be, if creepy beings like these have such things), and then use this to attach him to your cardboard hinge. Make sure you line up the folds neatly!

8 FINISHED!

Write in a birthday message (or any other occasion) and your pop-up card is ready to pop! How you decorate the front is up to you. May we suggest a nice, clear, friendly Minecraft landscape to lure the recipient into a false sense of security...?

WATCH THE LITTLE FELLA POP UP!

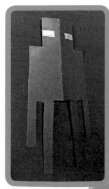

BARGAIN BUY!

MERCH CRAFT

The very best Minecraft loot money can buy

MIGHTY MINI FIGURES

These tiny figures are awesome for two reasons: 1. They're blind boxes, so you don't know which one you're going to get – if you unwrapped one of these cubes you'd get a double surprise; and 2. You won't run out of room, because they're adorably tiny! There's always the chance you'll end up with three of the same Minecart Steves, though, so finding friends to swap with might be a good idea.

CUSTOM ENDERTOY FIGURE

This might have to be the coolest Minecraft toy we've ever seen. Yes it's a simple figure, but it's also a completely customisable one. Want a collectable version of your favourite Minecraft YouTuber? Yep, they've got it. But the best thing of all is that if you put in your own username you can make a toy of yourself. Yes, you. Eeek! That's a pretty cool thing!

MAGNET SHEET

Someone else in the family hogging the TV so much that you can't play Minecraft? Well take over the fridge instead and build your own adventure scenes with these gorgeous magnets.

MAKE YOURSELF!

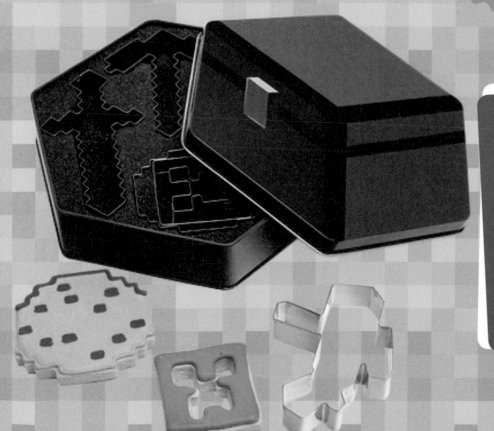

COOKIE CUTTERS

Make tasty, filling snacks for your Minecraft sessions with these appropriately shaped cookie cutters. They work really well with a simple sugar biscuit recipe, and while it can be a bit fiddly to get the dough out of the thin bits on the weapons, they hold their shape really well. All they need is plenty of green icing.

PAPER CRAFT SHELTER PACK

Want somewhere for all of your figures to live? Then these easy-to-build papercraft blocks are a great choice. They're made from sturdy card with clear folding instructions so you won't be left frustrated while building them. You can also mix and match with other sets to build some great custom projects. We've got ours set up as a background on a display shelf. Envy of the office, we are.

BARGAIN BUY!

LIGHT UP TORCH

This light up torch is a great way to turn any bedroom into your own Minecraft dungeon. Either hang it on your wall for that true mineshaft feeling, or carry it out into the wilderness to help illuminate your overworld adventures for real.

DIAMOND BRACELET

No, not that kind of diamond – this is a bargain buy after all. But even if doesn't sparkle as brightly as the real thing, it's still a fun little gift.

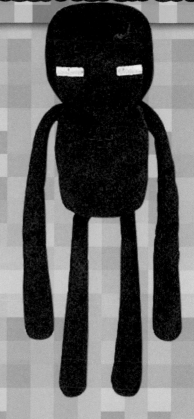

DIGGING WALL DECAL

To add to that bedroom/mineshaft feel, this wall sticker will make it look like you're digging into your own wall. Put up one of the light up torches on either side of it and you'll have your very own underground fortress. It might unnerve your folks or your landlord a tad, though...

ENDERMAN SOFT TOY

Look at his floppy little limbs! There are loads of different cuddly Minecraft toys you can buy, but the Enderman has a special place in our hearts as it feels like it's brimming with character and cute menace. Just don't look it in the eye...

ALEX FIGURE

With Steve merchandise being so easy to find, it's great to have a figure of his lady-faced counterpart Alex to go adventuring with. There are loads of other figures in the same style, and each one is really well made, too. They also work surprisingly well with the papercraft sets as backgrounds.

BARGAIN BUY!

GET MORE ROOM
Use Slabs for floors and ceilings to make even small rooms feel big. Super handy when you don't have much space for a build!

A CHIP OFF THE OLD BLOCK!

GET THE MOST OUT OF SLABS
Boost your builds by mastering these slab block tips

DETAILED ROOFS
It's not just stairs that can make your roof look great. Using Slabs to extend things out, or even as detail underneath makes your builds look even better.

REDSTONE HELP

Slabs work differently to blocks when it comes to making Redstone contraptions. They won't break circuits for starters.

LET ME HOP OVER AND TAKE A LOOK AT THAT!

BURY FURNITURE

Placing Slabs at the same levels as Beds and Chests makes them look buried and appear like your bed is on the floor. It's another great way to save space.

DECORATING

When combined with Stairs, Slabs can make all sorts of shapes, like this lion here made from two types of Sandstone.

MY HISS IS MORE SCARY THAN HIS ROAR!

STOP MOBS SPAWNING

Place Slabs on the bottom half of a block and mobs won't be able to spawn on them. Be careful though, if you place them in the top spot they do spawn.

LIGHT CAN PASS THROUGH THEM

Since they're not a full block, light can still pass through Slabs, which is handy when you want to have a build that doesn't use many Torches.

THE ULTIMATE MINECRAFT QUIZ!

PART 2

 31 Which piece of armour protects you the most?
A. Leggings
B. Helmet
C. Chestplate

32 How many types of Horse Armour are there?
A. 2
B. 3
C. 4

33 Which of these is NOT a Minecraft block?
A. Obsidian
B. Hay Bale
C. Marshmallow

34 What happens when you try to shoot an Enderman?
A. Your bow shoots out carrots instead of arrows
B. The Enderman teleports away before the arrow hits them
C. All Endermen turn around and attack you

35 Which of these is NOT a food in Minecraft?
A. Rabbit Stew
B. Mushroom Stew
C. Vegetable Stew

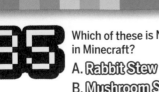

36 What happens when you eat a Pufferfish?

A. You get poisoned for a few seconds ◯

B. You turn into a Pufferfish ◯

C. You get a Water Breathing effect ◯

37 What happens when you walk on Soul Sand?

A. You walk much slower ◯

B. You walk much faster ◯

C. Nothing happens ◯

HOW ARE YOU DOING AT THE QUIZ? NO PEEKING AT THE ANSWERS AT THE BACK OF THE BOOK!

38 What is the default female skin called in Minecraft?

A. Sarah ◯

B. Alex ◯

C. Stephanie ◯

39 What happens when you hit a Llama?

A. It runs away ◯

B. It stands still and stares ◯

C. It spits at you ◯

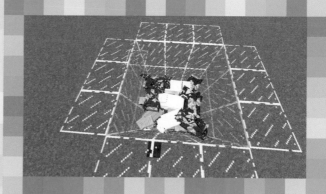

40 What happens when you name a mob 'Dinnerbone'?

A. It will fly away ◯

B. It will turn upside-down ◯

C. It will disappear ◯

41 How were Creepers invented?

A. Notch made a mistake while making Pigs ○

B. Someone asked Notch to make them ○

C. Creepers were supposed to be cactuses ○

42 What tool do you use for farming?

A. Pickaxe ○

B. Tractor ○

C. Hoe ○

43 What is the default male skin called in Minecraft?

A. Steve ○

B. Nick ○

C. Dave ○

44 What year was Minecraft officially released to the public?

A. 2009 ○

B. 2011 ○

C. 1987 ○

45 What type of tool must you mine Obsidian with?

A. Iron Pickaxe ○

B. Gold Pickaxe ○

C. Diamond Pickaxe ○

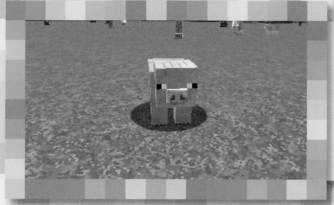

46 What happens when a Pig is struck by lightning?

A. It turns into cooked Porkchops

B. It pops and flies away

C. It turns into a Zombie Pigman

47 What is the name of the naturally spawning mob that lives in villages?

A. Villager

B. Pig

C. Sheep

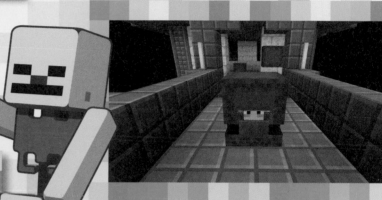

48 Which mob is found inside an End City?

A. End Person

B. Bat

C. Shulker

49 What is the name of the mob that is summoned with 2 Snow Blocks and 1 Pumpkin?

A. Iron Golem

B. Snow Golem

C. Frosty the Snowman

50 What block can be crafted with Sand and Gunpowder?

A. Fireworks

B. Gravel

C. TNT

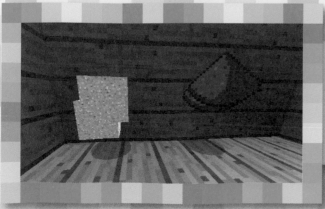

ANSWERS ON PAGE **93**

KNOW YOUR BIOMES
#5 DESERT

IF A DESERT IS NEXT TO THE OCEAN OR A RIVER BIOME, YOU WILL FIND SUGAR CANE GROWS IN IT! SUGAR CANE IS AN IMPORTANT INGREDIENT IN MANY CRAFTING RECIPES.

A DESERT IS THE ONLY PLACE IN MINECRAFT WHERE DESERT VILLAGES, DESERT TEMPLES AND DESERT WELLS WILL APPEAR.

JUST LIKE IN real life, the Desert biome is a very dry, barren place where you won't find much growing. It's just full of sand dunes and a lot of cacti! It is a great place for mining Sandstone though – it is found just underneath the surface. With its wide open spaces, the Desert is a place where you can see hostile mobs coming from a mile away. Well that's handy!

THERE'S JUST ONE MOB THAT SPAWNS NATURALLY IN THE DESERT – THE GOLD RABBIT. IT IS VERY WELL CAMOUFLAGED AGAINST THE SAND. THERE MIGHT BE 100 IN THIS PICTURE – YOU WOULD NEVER KNOW!

BE SURE TO STOCK UP ON FOOD AND TOOLS BEFORE VISITING THE DESERT, AS THERE'S NOTHING TO FEED ON ONCE YOU GET HERE – JUST LOTS AND LOTS OF SAND!

HOW TO FIND THE...
RAREST MOBS!

They're out there if you're feeling lucky

> I'M NOT A ZOMBIE, I'M A HEN-DERMAN!

1 CHICKEN JOCKEY

Finding Baby Zombies and Baby Zombie Pigmen can be tough enough, but there's a 5% chance that when they spawn they'll do so on a Chicken! To increase your chances of seeing one, spawn normal Chickens near Baby Zombies and they might just ride them.
Found in: PC, Console, Pocket Edition

2 ENDERMITE

Every time you use an Enderpearl there's a 5% chance you'll spawn an Endermite. They might be small and despawn quickly, but they can be tough to hit because of their size.
Found in: PC, Console

3 SPIDER JOCKEY

Every Spider has a 1% chance of having a Skeleton on it when it spawns, so you'll have to do lots of searching to find one. You also won't find any during the day even though they ride Spiders – the Skeleton part still burns in the sun, leaving the Spider behind unharmed.
Found in: PC, Console, Pocket Edition

4 CHARGED CREEPER

You know you need to run when you hear a Creeper hiss, but you'll need to run even further if it's a Charged Creeper as they have an even bigger explosion. If lightning hits a normal Creeper it supercharges it, making it twice as powerful. It'll also make any nearby mobs drop their heads.
Found in: PC, Console, Pocket Edition

6 SKELETON HORSEMAN

If you see a Skeleton Horse be wary – it's a trap! These Horses are super rare, but if you do find one don't step within 10 blocks of it if you're not ready to fight. Get close and it'll be struck by lightning, turning it into not 1, but 4 Skeleton Horsemen with enchanted bows.
Found in: PC, Pocket Edition

5 OVERWORLD PIGMAN

Finding a Zombie Pigman in the Nether is easy, but did you know that they can spawn in the Overworld too? If lightning strikes within 4 blocks of a Pig then it'll turn into a Zombie Pigman, but the chances of it being close enough is really low.
Found in: PC, Console, Pocket Edition

Make it! XMAS BAUBLE

When it comes to trimming the tree, you can't beat the humble bauble. Bright, dangly and festive, it's got your decoration needs covered in one handy item. Here we'll show you how to make a simple Creeper's head bauble with just a few materials – and trust us, it's nowhere near as tricky as it sounds!

YOU'LL NEED...

Square of green paper or cardboard (paper folds more easily, but card will hold its shape better – we used 21x21cm), black glitter glue, green thread, sellotape, scissors

INFO

ORIGAMI XMAS BAUBLE

DIFFICULTY: EASY TO TRICKY
TIME NEEDED: 20 MINS
TELL MUM? YES – YOU MAY NEED HELP WITH THE SCISSORS!

1 FOLD TO BEGIN

Fold two opposite corners of your paper together diagonally, then unfold it and do the same with the other two corners. If your paper is only coloured on one side, make sure you do this with the coloured side facing down. You want to make sure that your folds are as sharp as possible throughout, so don't be afraid to go over them a few times with your fingernail. Turn your paper over, fold one pair of edges together, unfold, and do the same with the other two edges. Got it?

HERE'S WHAT YOUR FOLDED SHEET SHOULD LOOK LIKE!

2 HOLE PUNCHER

When you unfold your sheet, you should now be able to see that all four of the fold lines meet at a single point in the centre. Use the point of your scissors to pierce a small hole at this point – be careful of your fingers, mind, as you'll be needing them! Snip off a 10cm piece of thread, and fold it in half to make a loop. Thread the ends through the hole you've just made, and stick them in place on the diagonally folded side with some sellotape. This will hang your bauble when it's done.

POKE THE TWO ENDS THROUGH TO MAKE A HANGER!

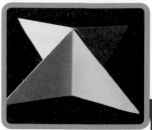

NOW PAY ATTENTION!

With this loop facing upwards, carefully fold your paper along the diagonal lines you made before, pinching it into place as you go. The two sets of folds should collapse together, leaving you with one large triangle. The pair of points at the bottom end of your triangle will be in two layers. Lift the top layer, and bring the points up towards the top of the triangle. Fold them into place. Now bring their outside corners into the middle and fold them into place.

THIS BIT SOUNDS TRICKY, BUT IT WILL MAKE SENSE SOON!

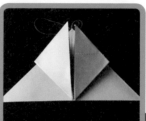

WORLD OF FOLDS

Fold the top points down into the middle, then fold them back on themselves, so that they're pointing outwards. Now open them back out slightly, and tuck them securely into the little pocket that's right underneath them. This is the fiddliest bit, so don't worry if it takes you a while to get it perfect! And if you're not so good with your fingers, ask for help. Flip your paper shape over and repeat steps 4 and 5 on the other side. You should end up with a slightly wonky hexagon. Don't worry: that means you're doing it right!

FINISHING TOUCHES

Pick up your wonky hexagon, and you'll find a small hole at the bottom. Blow gently into it and your bauble will inflate, like magic, taking shape as a cube. It's a Christmas miracle! Feel free to gently pinch along the edges to give more definition to the shape. Now it's time to decorate your bauble by painting a Creeper face on it with glitter glue. If your glue's nozzle isn't great for fiddly work, you can always use a small paintbrush to add the features. Let it dry overnight, and it's ready to hang on your tree. Ka-boom!

HERE HE IS, ALL PUFFED UP AND READY TO BLOW!

PUZZLES

Test your brains with these teasers...

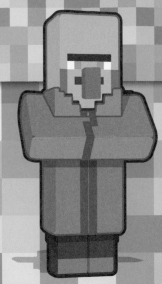

ANSWERS ON PAGE 93

SPOT THE DIFFERENCE

CAN YOU spot all ten changes we made to the pic?

SPOT THE DIFFERENCE ON THIS IMAGE...

I COUNTED

DIFFERENCES

QUICK BUILD!

Build a cannon to launch chickens at your friends!

5 MINUTES!

START HERE!

1 USE any block you like, plus one Piston block to build this shape. Make sure you build it sort of high up so your Chickens will shoot out further.

2 ADD a row of blocks on top of that all the way around the edge, then put a Lever on the block above the Piston. Use the Lever so the Piston blocks the cannon.

3 LOAD your Chickens! Spawn loads of them, as many as you can, all in that one free square. Once you think you have enough put a block on top so they don't escape.

4 NOW push the Lever again and they should all fire out! It works really well on Pocket Edition.

BUILD THIS!

KNOW YOUR BIOMES
#6 SWAMPLAND

NEED SOME CLAY OR DIRT BLOCKS? YOU WILL FIND THEM AT THE BOTTOM OF THE POOLS OF WATER IN THE SWAMPLANDS. YOU'LL HAVE TO HOLD YOUR BREATH TO MINE THEM!

FORAGING AROUND THE SWAMP YOU WILL FIND A LOT OF MUSHROOMS AND SUGARCANE. IF YOU'RE PLAYING THE POCKET EDITION GIANT MUSHROOMS WILL GROW TOO – YOU'LL GET LOTS OF STEW FROM THEM!

FASCINATING BY DAY, dangerous by night, the Swamplands are a mixture of flat dry blocks at water level, with pools of green water and lily pads floating on it. The mixture of temperatures makes dark green vines grow on trees, mushrooms grow like crazy and the colours of all the plants vary. In the Pocket Edition the water is even a grey colour, instead of blue.

SLIMES JUST LOVE IT IN THE SWAMPS! THEY WILL SPAWN NATURALLY AT NIGHT-TIME, AND WILL SPREAD LIKE WILDFIRE ON A FULL MOON! THIS MAKES THE SWAMP A VERY DANGEROUS PLACE TO BE AT NIGHT.

THE ONLY PLACE A WITCH'S HUT WILL GENERATE IN MINECRAFT IS IN THE SWAMPLANDS. INSIDE YOU WILL FIND AN EMPTY CAULDRON, A CRAFTING TABLE AND A FLOWER POT. WHAT ARE THEY UP TO?

Make it!
SPIDER CUPCAKES

You can find me on the web!

SPIDER CUPCAKES

DIFFICULTY: NORMAL
TIME NEEDED: 45 MINUTES
TELL MUM? IF YOU'RE USING SHARP KNIVES TO CUT STUFF!

Get revenge for being pounced on in the dark by munching on a spidery treat!

INGREDIENTS

100g plain flour, 140g caster sugar, 20g cocoa powder, 1½ tsp baking powder, 120ml milk, one large egg, vanilla extract, 190g butter (take it out of the fridge about an hour before you start), 450g icing sugar, black food dye, red wine gums, liquorice sticks, icing bag, plain dark-coloured cake cases, 12-hole muffin tin

1 MASTER THE MIX

Set your oven to 170º (or 150º if you have a fan oven) and leave it to heat up while you're making your cake mix. Boring, but important, that. In a large bowl, mix together your flour, sugar, cocoa powder, baking powder and 40g of the butter, until it looks a bit like chocolatey grit. If you have a mixer, this stage will be much easier – but it's still possible to do it with a wooden spoon and some patience!

THIS STEP CAN GET REALLLLLY MESSY!

WARNING
ASK A GROWN UP TO HELP YOU USE THE OVEN, THEY ARE VERY HOT! STAY SAFE.

2 GET IT TOGETHER

Crack in your egg, add a small splash of vanilla essence and mix it together – then add the milk a little bit at a time. Don't worry if the batter you end up with seems runnier than a normal cake mix – you'll end up with lovely, light cupcakes this way.

3 POUR OUT A DOZEN

Put a cake case in each of your tin's holes, and then carefully divide your cake mix between the 12 cases. They won't be full right to the top, but this leaves them enough space to rise. Bake them for around 25 minutes – you can tell when they're done by popping a sharp knife into the middle of one of the cakes and seeing if it comes out clean. Let them cool completely before you ice them.

TRY NOT TO EAT THEM ALL BEFORE THEY'VE COOLED!

MAKE SURE YOU DON'T GET THIS STUFF ON YOUR CLOTHES!

4 PAINT IT BLACK

Mix the remaining 150g of butter with the icing sugar until it forms a creamy icing – you might need to add a splash of milk or water to loosen it up a bit, but make sure you only put in a tiny bit at a time! Mix in your food dye until you get a deep black colour. Food dye tends to be stronger than food colouring, so start off slowly (and make sure you stick to the guidelines on the bottle for the maximum recommended amount).

5 BEGIN TO DECORATE!

Fill a disposable piping bag with your icing, and snip a V shape in the end – make it about 1cm across. Use the bag to pipe a thick swirl of icing on the top of each cake. Don't worry if it doesn't look perfect, as you'll be putting decorations on top as well!

IT'S A WHOLE ARMY OF SPIDERS! HELLLLLP!

THIS MAKES THE BODY OF YOUR SPIDER

6 MAKE THE EYES AND LEGS

Cut your red wine gums into small squares for eyes (you'll need two per cake, so 24 in total), and snip your liquorice sticks into 'legs' a few centimetres long (eight legs per cake means a whopping 96 of these). Arrange these various body parts on top of each cupcake, and enjoy your deliciously spooky handiwork!

PIXEL SNAKES & LADDERS

Grab some counters and a dice then race to the finish in our Pixel Snakes & Ladders game!

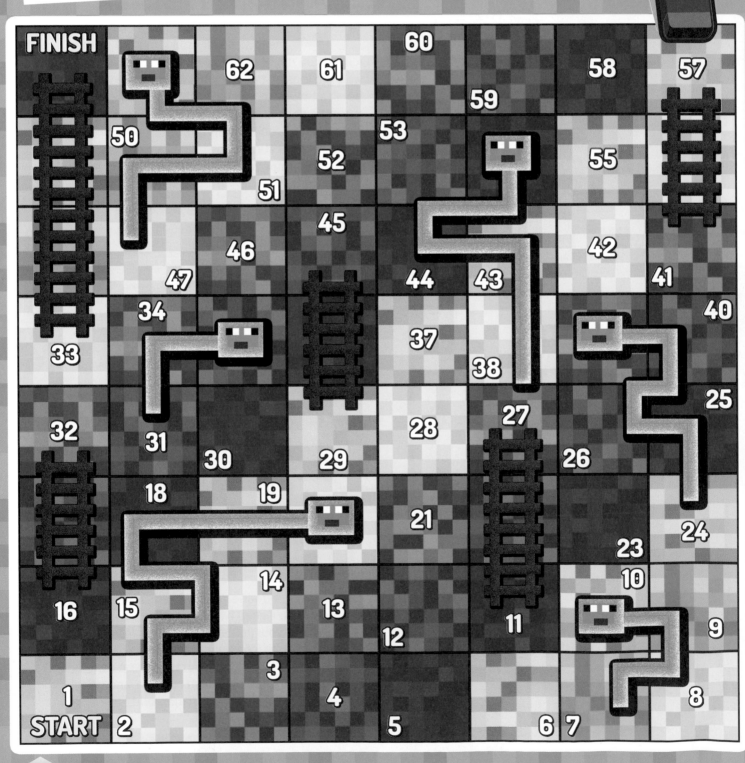

Speech bubble: HEY, ENDERMAN! HOW DO YOU READ A BOOK?

Speech bubble: I LIKE TO START AT THE END!

GAMES MASTER
PRESENTS
MINECRAFT

TIPS CARDS!
CUT OUT AND KEEP EXPERT TIPS CARDS

BLOCK — Emerald Ore

THIS mineral block is the rarest in the whole of Minecraft. It will drop one **Emerald** per ore when mined, which can be used to trade with villagers for unique items. They are most commonly found under the highest hills.

ITEM — Book

YOU will need **3 Paper** and **1 Leather** item in your inventory to craft yourself a **Book**. Find a **Bookshelf** and mine this, or blow it up, and **3 Books** will be dropped unless you have the **Silk Touch** enchantment active.

MOB — Chicken

GRASSY areas are the places to find **Chickens**, they generate anywhere there is **Grass** and lots of space above. **Chickens** are the only mobs in Minecraft to lay **Eggs**, useful if you want to bake **Cakes**!

WEAPON — Bow

THERE are various ways you can get yourself a **Bow**. You can Craft one using **3 Sticks** and **3 Strings**, you can catch one while **Fishing**, you can **Trade** one with a Villager or a **Skeleton** has an 8.5% chance of dropping one!

FOOD — Mushroom Stew

GRAB an empty **Bowl** and milk a **Mooshroom** by using the **Bowl** on it to get a **Bowl** of steaming hot **Mushroom Stew**. Eating this will restore **6 Hunger** points in one go, and also be quite delicious!

VEHICLE — Minecart

ATTACK a **Minecart** for ages and eventually you will get to keep it, adding it to your **Inventory**. Careful though, if you attack with a **Sword** or **Bow** you will destroy it! Minecarts are loads of fun!

MINECRAFT TIPS CARDS!

WHY NOT CUT OUT THE CARDS AND PLAY A TOP TRUMPS-STYLE GAME?!

▶ BECOME A MINECRAFT EXPERT!

GET YOUR safety scissors at the ready because we've created eight pages of Minecraft tips cards especially for you. 33 cards in total, written by Minecraft experts. Covering Blocks, Items, Mobs, Weapons, Food, Vehicles and more! All you need to do is cut them out by carefully cutting along the dotted lines (round off the corners if you like). Then keep them handy the next time you play!

MINECRAFT TIPS CARDS!

Chicken

- IF you throw an Egg there is a 1-in-8 chance of it becoming a Chicken. There's then a 1-in-32 chance it will spawn 4 Chickens!

- TO breed Chickens, tap 2 that are close with the Seeds from Wheat, Beetroot, Pumpkin or Melon. On the console game, you can also use Nether Wart.

- Chicken Jockeys are a very rare sight – a Baby Zombie or Baby Zombie Pigman riding on a Chicken!

MINECRAFT TIPS CARDS!

Book

- YOU can write your own Books in Minecraft by using a Book, an Ink Sac and a Feather. Build a Bookshelf with Books and Wood Planks.

- TAKE your Book to an Enchantment Table to turn it into an Enchanted Book. Use these on tools and weapons to give that enchantment.

- IF you find yourself with a lot of Books, you can sell them to Librarian Villagers. They will buy 8-10 books for an Emerald.

MINECRAFT TIPS CARDS!

Emerald Ore

- YOU will generally find this block between levels 4 and 32 in the Minecraft world.

- IF playing on the computer edition, you will need an Iron or Diamond Pickaxe to mine Emerald Ore.

- POCKET Edition players can also use a Stone Pickaxe to mine this precious block.

- EMERALDS were going to be rubies, until the team at Mojang decided they were too close to Redstone.

MINECRAFT TIPS CARDS!

Minecart

- WATCH out while riding in a Minecart if there are Cacti about – they will explode on impact.

- CRAFTING is a fun way of making your own Minecarts, use 5 Iron Ingots to get one.

- YOU can place a Minecart like any other block, but place it on a Rail to make it more useful.

- JUMP into a Minecart and press Use to set it rolling. Jump out again by pressing the Sneak button.

MINECRAFT TIPS CARDS!

Mushroom Stew

- IT'S fun to milk a Mooshroom, but you can also get Mushroom Stew by crafting with a Red Mushroom, a Brown Mushroom and a Bowl.

- ONCE you have eaten your Mushroom Stew, the empty Bowl will be returned to your Inventory.

- DON'T think you can stack up a pile of Mushroom Stew Bowls for a feast though, this used to work in version 1.2.5, but has been changed to give a single Bowl of stew.

MINECRAFT TIPS CARDS!

Bow

- FIRING an Arrow from a Bow at full strength at the perfect angle, may travel up to 120 Blocks.

- TO use a Bow you must have at least 1 Arrow in your Inventory and it is drawn back by simply using it.

- ARROWS are effective weapons, unless you are shooting an Enderman, they will teleport away.

- ENCHANT a Bow with Infinity and you will never run out of Arrows, or try Flame for Flaming Arrows.

ARMOUR — Chain Helmet

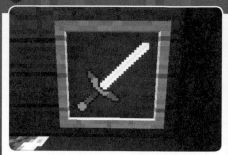

IF YOU want to protect your head then luckily there are five types of **Helmet** in Minecraft. This Chain Helmet isn't the **strongest**, but will increase your **Defense points by 2**. It also looks great on!

UTILITY — Bed

THE bed is actually just **1 block**, and when used to go to sleep it will **reset your spawn point** to nearby. Beds come in a multitude of colours and can be Crafted using **3 matching Wool** blocks and **3 Wood Planks** of any type.

DECOR — Item Frame

YOU'VE seen those 'Break glass in case of emergency' signs, right? Well this is Minecraft's equivalent. You can put any item inside an **Item Frame**, then when you need it just **punch the frame** and it will drop out!

BLOCK — Water

IT'S a natural part of the **Overworld**, so water will be everywhere – streams, rivers, lakes, seas – as well as in wells in villages. You can't pick it up as an item, but you can fill a bucket with water to use elsewhere.

ITEM — Spawn Eggs

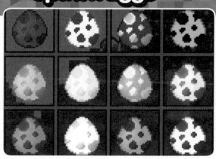

THE **Spawn Egg** is only available in **Creative Mode**, not **Survival**, and each egg spawns an animal into the world. There are 30 in the console game, 37 in Pocket Edition and 42 in the computer version of Minecraft.

MOB — Wither

SPAWNING **Withers** is done by making a T shape out of **Soul Sand** then placing **Wither Skeleton Skulls** on top of the **3 top blocks**. It works in all modes except for **Peaceful**, as Withers are anything but peaceful!

WEAPON — Wooden Sword

THE most basic of Swords you can craft, using any **Wooden Planks** and a **Stick**. They can block attacks but are not as effective in a battle as the **Stone**, **Iron** or **Diamond Swords**. Bizarrely, they are as good as **Gold Swords**.

FOOD — Spider Eye

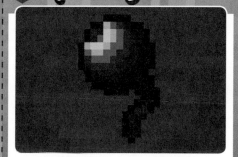

WHEN **Spiders** (or **Cave Spiders** – they live in caves!) are killed by you they will drop a **Spider Eye**, but not if they're killed in a natural way. They are a kind of food, but are poisonous if you try to eat it. So don't.

VEHICLE — Boat

THERE are six different types of **Boat**, depending on the **Wooden Planks** you use to craft one: **Oak**, **Spruce**, **Birch**, **Jungle**, **Acacia** and **Dark Oak**. There's no difference between their use though, so pick your favourite!

MINECRAFT TIPS CARDS!

Item Frame

- **CRAFTING** an Item Frame can be done by combining 8 Sticks and 1 Leather together.
- **THERE** is only one naturally generating Item Frame in the game – on an End Ship containing Elytra.
- **PLACE** a Map inside an Item Frame and the Map will enlarge to show your location with a green pointer.
- **THE** Achievement 'Map Room' can be earned by placing 9 Maps in Item Frames in a 3x3 square.

MINECRAFT TIPS CARDS!

Bed

- **YOU** don't always have to Craft your bed, they do naturally generate in the world too – inside Igloos in the icy biomes.
- **GO** to sleep in a Bed by pressing the Use button. You can only sleep at night-time though, unless there's a thunderstorm going on!
- **BEFORE** you face The End or The Nether, get plenty of sleep. Placing a Bed there will make it explode if you try to sleep in it!

MINECRAFT TIPS CARDS!

Chain Helmet

- **THERE** are five types of Helmet in the game: Leather Cap, Chain Helmet, Iron, Diamond & Gold.
- **IF** you have two Helmets that are damaged, you can Craft them both together to create one good one.
- **BADLY** damaged Helmets can often be picked up from defeated mobs like Zombies or Skeletons in armour.
- **YOU** can use Enchantments on Helmets to increase their usefulness in battles.

MINECRAFT TIPS CARDS!

Wither

- **IF** you manage to kill a Wither it will drop a Nether Star. You can use the Nether Star to craft Beacons.
- **THE** Looting enchantment does not work on the Wither, so you will still get only one Nether Star.
- **WHEN** it first spawns the Wither will flash blue and get bigger as its health bar fills up, it is completely invulnerable when this is happening. Watch out when it's done expanding – there will be a large explosion!

MINECRAFT TIPS CARDS!

Spawn Eggs

- **YOU** can press the Pick Block button on any mob you like to obtain its Spawn Egg. Use the Egg on the same mob and you will create a baby version.
- **WHEN** spawning Horses you will get a Horse 90% of the time, but 10% of the time it will be a Donkey.
- **SPAWNING** Rabbits gives you mobs with random skins. If you want black and white Rabbits you need to rename the Egg 'Toast' on an Anvil.

MINECRAFT TIPS CARDS!

Water

- **WHEN** there is water around it will spread into every close by Air block, continuing to flow until contained.
- **IT** will wash away many things in its path – Plants, Cobwebs, Redstone, Rails, Torches and put out Fires.
- **IN** the snowy biomes water will turn into Ice blocks when it freezes. When it melts it turns back again.
- **DIVING** under water will reduce the amount of light by 2 for every block you go deeper down.

MINECRAFT TIPS CARDS!

Boat

- **CONSOLE** players can craft a Boat with 5 matching Wood Planks while Pocket Edition players must use 5 matching Wood Planks and a Wooden Shovel to act as the oar.
- **PRESS** the Item button to get into a Boat, then Sneak to get back out (Leave Boat on Pocket).
- **YOU** control a Boat with the direction controls, keys on the PC games or the on-screen controls that pop up on Pocket Edition.

MINECRAFT TIPS CARDS!

Spider Eye

- **FOR** every Spider killed you will receive 1 Spider Eye. Killing Witches will actually give you 6.
- **CRAFTING** a Spider Eye with Brown Mushroom and Sugar will give you a Fermented Spider Eye that can be used to make Negative Effect Potions or the Potion of Invisibility.
- **EATING** a Spider Eye will restore 2 Hunger Points and 3.2 Saturation Points with Nourishment of 1.6. But it will also poison you for 4 seconds.

MINECRAFT TIPS CARDS!

Wooden Sword

- **YOU** can use a Sword to destroy blocks more quickly than using your fists alone, but unbreakable blocks will decrease durability.
- **WHEN** playing Survival Mode you can earn an achievement when you make your first Wooden Sword, it's called 'Time to Strike!'
- **IF** you are fed up with the limitations of your Wooden Sword, you can always throw it into a Furnace and use it as fuel!

ARMOUR — Iron Chestplate

PROTECTING your upper body, the Iron Chestplate is stronger than Gold, Leather or Chainmail, but not as strong as Diamond. A Blacksmith will sell you one for 10-14 Emeralds. Craft one with 8 Iron Ingots.

UTILITY — Brewing Stand

MAKING up a single block, a Brewing Stand is used for brewing Potions, Splash Potions and Lingering Potions. They can be Crafted combining a Blaze Rod and 3 blocks of Cobblestone together.

DECOR — Music Disc

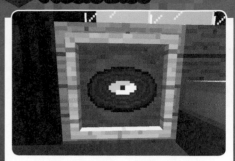

MINECRAFT has its own built-in music to enjoy. Using a Jukebox you can play these Music Discs, seen here in an Item Frame. There are 12 tunes in total, created by Daniel Rosenfeld, otherwise known as C418.

BLOCK — Bedrock

WHILE playing in Survival Mode, Bedrock can't be broken with any tools, moved by Pistons or destroyed by explosions. It's the base underneath your world. You can only obtain it in Creative Mode.

ITEM — Blaze Rod

BLAZES will drop Blaze Rods when you kill them, or they are killed by a tamed Wolf. If they are killed by any other means, they won't drop one. They are used in a variety of Crafting recipes as a fuel.

MOB — Llama

ONLY a recent addition to Minecraft, Llamas are great as they can be tamed and used to carry lots of items in one go. These neutral mobs spawn in Savanna and Extreme Hills biomes in herds of four or five.

WEAPON — Snowball

BREAK up a Snow block and you will get Snowballs! These throwable items are great fun for snowball fights in multiplayer Minecraft games. You can turn 4 Snowballs back into a Snow block by Crafting them.

FOOD — Bread

FANCY a sandwich? You can find Bread in over a third of all chests as one of the main food items in Minecraft. There are often multiple loaves in one chest. Alternatively, Craft some bread with 3 Wheat.

VEHICLE — Elytra

MADE famous in the new Glide mini-game on console, Elytra (or Elytra Wings in Pocket Edition) allow you to glide around the world with a giant pair of wings on your back. You only find them in End Cities.

MINECRAFT TIPS CARDS!

Music Disc

- WHILE there are 12 default Music Discs in the game, these can be changed using Resource Packs.
- IF you kill a Creeper with a Skeleton's Arrow it will drop a random Music Disc.
- THE 12 Music Discs have titles like 'Blocks', 'Mellohi', 'Strad' and 'Cat'. They are a mix of musical styles.
- PLAYING your first Music Disc in the console game will earn you the 'Music To My Ears' Achievement.

MINECRAFT TIPS CARDS!

Brewing Stand

- YOU can find naturally generating Brewing Stands in End City ships, the basement of Igloos and sometimes in Witch's Huts found in Swampland biomes.
- PRESS Use on a Brewing Stand to start it, it is fuelled by Blaze Powder, 1 piece gives 20 attempts at brewing.
- TO brew yourself a Potion you need to combine the ingredients, Blaze Powder and a Bottle.

MINECRAFT TIPS CARDS!

Iron Chestplate

- YOU can double the durability of damaged matching Chestplates by Crafting them together, you even get a bonus 5% durability on top.
- OVER a quarter of all Blacksmiths chests will have an Iron Chestplate inside them. 12% of Stronghold altar chests will also have one.
- YOU activate a Chestplate by placing it in the second armour slot in your inventory. An Iron Chestplate will take 241 damage.

MINECRAFT TIPS CARDS!

Llama

- YOU will find that a Llama's wool colour will change depending on which biome it comes from.
- TAMING a Llama is done by tapping them until they show hearts, then you can ride them.
- YOU'RE in for a crazy ride though – you can't control where the Llama goes, just hang on!
- ATTACH a Lead to a Llama and not only will that one follow you, but others around will too in a caravan!

MINECRAFT TIPS CARDS!

Blaze Rod

- TO get yourself a Blaze Rod you will have to visit The Nether – it's the only place where Blazes are found.
- BREWING Stands are Crafted by mixing a Blaze Rod with 3 Cobblestone blocks.
- WHEN used as a fuel in a Furnace, the Blaze Rod will burn brightly for 120 seconds.
- YOU can earn the Achievement 'Into Fire' the first time you take a Blaze Rod away from a Blaze!

MINECRAFT TIPS CARDS!

Bedrock

- THE bottom 5 layers of the Overworld are made from Bedrock, with a jagged pattern.
- BEDROCK in The Nether is actually the top and bottom 4 layers of the world – there's no escape that way!
- THE Ender Crystal is made up of Bedrock that remains even after the crystal has been destroyed.
- WHEN you kill the Ender Dragon, End Gateway Portals are made – these are also Bedrock.

MINECRAFT TIPS CARDS!

Elytra

- THE wings are grey in colour usually, but if you are wearing a cape they will take on that colour.
- WITH the Elytra equipped in the Chestplate slot, jump when in mid-air to start a glide.
- NOT fast enough for you? Try holding a Firework Rocket in your hand while gliding – whoosh!
- YOU get 7 minutes and 11 seconds of gliding time before the durability of your wings gives up.

MINECRAFT TIPS CARDS!

Bread

- VILLAGER Farmers will sell Bread to you, for 2-4 Bread you will have to pay 1 Emerald.
- EATING a piece of Bread will restore 5 Hunger points and 6 Hunger Saturation points.
- THE Achievement 'Bake Bread' can be earned in all versions of the game by crafting 3 Wheat into Bread.
- BREAD is stackable in Chests, so you can stash lots of it in your home for scoffing later on!

MINECRAFT TIPS CARDS!

Snowball

- WHEN you throw a Snowball it is affected by gravity, so will drop over a long distance.
- SNOWBALLS do little damage to mobs, but they will knock them back giving you getaway time!
- THEY are most powerful when thrown at End Crystals – they completely destroy them!
- SNOW Golems will drop up to 15 Snowballs when they die. Great for stocking up!

ARMOUR — Diamond Leggings

IF it's your legs you want to protect then you're going to need some **armoured Leggings**. The toughest you can find in the game are the **Diamond Leggings**. Much better than the flimsy Leather Pants!

UTILITY — Saddle

IF you want to go for a ride on a mob in Minecraft you're going to need to place a **Saddle** on them first! You can **Trade** one from **Leatherworker Villagers** for **8-10 Emeralds**, or find one on your travels.

DECOR — Zombie Head

IF a nasty mob gets blown up in a **Charged Creeper explosion** they will drop their head! You can then pick up the head and wear it as a **disguise!** Above we're wearing a Zombie Head, great for sneaking through Zombies!

BLOCK — Ladder

MADE from **Wood**, the Ladder is a very useful block if you want to climb to the top of some other blocks! They can be **attached to the side of blocks**. Notch didn't want Ladders in Minecraft, but the fans demanded it!

ITEM — Rabbit's Foot

KILLING a Rabbit will result in a **10% chance** of it dropping a Rabbit's Foot when dead. They are known to be lucky charms, but in Minecraft they are also used as a **Brewing ingredient** for Potions.

MOB — Snow Golem

HAVING one of these Snow Golem around to protect you is a good idea. They are known as **Utility mobs**, which means they can be useful in defending against **hostile mobs**. They are also known as **Snowmen**.

TOOL — Fire Charge

NEED to start a fire? Well one way to do it is with a **Fire Charge**. It's useful to have a few of these in your inventory, you can Craft them by combining **Blaze Powder with Coal** or **Gunpowder with Charcoal**.

FOOD — Pumpkin Pie

MIX together **Pumpkin, Sugar and Egg** and you get yourself a **Pumpkin Pie!** Of course, if you're rubbish at cooking then you can always go to a village where a **Villager Farmer** will sell you one for an **Emerald**.

TOOL — Iron Shovel

IF you're mining for blocks, the most important tool in the box is the **Shovel**. Iron Shovels are very durable, giving **251 Uses** before they break, Stone ones give 132, Wood ones 60, Gold ones 33 and Diamond 1,562!

MINECRAFT
TIPS CARDS!

Zombie Head

- WEARING a Zombie Head is a great way to break the ice at a party, but it does have a useful purpose too...
- YOU can sneak through a pack of Zombies in disguise with one of these on your head! They are 50% less likely to spot you.
- THEY can also be used in Crafting. Combine a Zombie Head with Gunpowder and any Dye to make a Firework that explodes in the shape of a Creeper – cool!

MINECRAFT
TIPS CARDS!

Saddle

- SADDLES are found in Chests in varying numbers. Nether Fortresses have the most, followed by Desert Temples and Dungeons.
- THE other way you can find a Saddle is through Fishing! Occasionally you'll hook one instead of a fish!
- PIGS, Mules, Donkeys and Horses can have a Saddle used on them to make them controllable when you ride. To control a Pig you will also need a Carrot on a Stick!

MINECRAFT
TIPS CARDS!

Diamond Leggings

- SEVEN Diamonds can be Crafted together to make yourself a pair of Diamond Leggings.
- THERE is a slim chance that Skeletons, Zombie Pigmen or Zombies will drop Leggings on death.
- PLACE armoured Leggings in the third armour slot in your inventory to use them.
- DIAMOND Leggings are very durable with a value of 496, compared to 76 for Leather ones.

MINECRAFT
TIPS CARDS!

Snow Golem

- YOU can make yourself a Snow Golem by placing 2 Snow blocks either one on top of the other, or side by side, then placing either a Pumpkin or Jack o'lantern next to it.
- SNOW Golems can form naturally in the world if a Pumpkin Stem grows next to 2 Snow blocks. This happens most frequently in the Ice Spikes biome where Pumpkins grow close to the snow. When you kill them they will drop 15 Snowballs.

MINECRAFT
TIPS CARDS!

Rabbit's Foot

- MAKING a Mundane Potion, that you can later use in creating more exciting Potions, is done by mixing a Rabbit's Foot with a Water Bottle.
- MORE excitingly, a Potion of Leaping is brewed up by mixing a Rabbit's Foot with an Awkward Potion. Drink one of these and you will be able to jump higher in the air and take less damage when falling back down to the ground.

MINECRAFT
TIPS CARDS!

Ladder

- HOUSES in Villages that have fences outside will have Ladders inside, along with Churches.
- IGLOOS also have Ladders, but this time they lead down into the basement, they're also on End Ships.
- A nearby Ladder can save your life! If falling, edge close to one, it will slow down your rate of descent.
- IF you are fed up with your Ladders you can use them as Fuel instead – they can Smelt 1.5 items each.

MINECRAFT
TIPS CARDS!

Iron Shovel

- USING a Shovel will allow you to break some blocks faster in the game, but each one you break will reduce the durability of the Shovel.
- YOU can use a Shovel on Grass blocks to make yourself a Grass pathway.
- IF you are low on weapons while being attacked by hostile mobs, a Shovel will do nicely! Attacking with one in your hand will cause 2 Damage to the Shovel.

MINECRAFT
TIPS CARDS!

Pumpkin Pie

- AS Pumpkin Pies are easily stackable, they are useful food items to keep around. Eating a pie will restore 4.8 saturation points and 8 hunger points.
- TO eat a Pumpkin Pie, equip it in the hotbar and press the Use button. Then wipe your chin.
- PUMPKIN Pies are useful for earning the 'Husbandry' and 'A Balanced Diet' Advancements where you need to eat certain foods!

MINECRAFT
TIPS CARDS!

Fire Charge

- YOU can use Fire Charges as ammunition in Dispensers to send out fireballs on demand.
- THEY can be used in a similar way to Flint and Steel, starting a fire instantly when you use them.
- AS they are easily storable, Fire Charges are handy to have for use as Crafting ingredients.
- USING a Fire Charge will destroy it. They can be used to prime TNT blocks. Stand well back!

PUZZLES

Test your brains with these teasers...

I WONDER IF I'M IN THE CREEPER SEARCH?

ANSWERS ON PAGE 93

CREEPER SEARCH

FORGET BORING wordsearches – this is the **Creeper Search**! We've hidden **11 Minecraft words** in the face of the Creeper below. Can you find them all?

S	P	R	U	C	E	X	T	N	P
R	I	B	L	A	Z	E	I	N	O
R	G			K	C			W	T
E	M			E	B			I	A
D	A	K	R			O	O	T	T
S	N	B				N	H	O	
T	E	R				T	E	X	
O	S	I		S	T	H	R	E	
N	E	T	H	E	R	B	E	S	R
E	C	R	E	E	P	E	R	W	O

KNOW YOUR BIOMES
#7 ICE PLAINS

APART FROM POLAR BEARS, THE OTHER BIG DANGER IN THE ICE PLAINS ARE THE STRAYS. THESE ARE SKELETONS THAT HAVE SPAWNED UNDER THE ICY COLD SKY, ARMED WITH BOWS AND ARROWS THAT WILL INFLICT SLOWNESS FOR 30 SECONDS IF YOU GET SHOT.

ON THE WILD AND COLD OPEN ICY PLAINS YOU WILL COME ACROSS BLACK AND WHITE RABBITS, BUT THE MAIN ANIMAL AROUND THESE PARTS IS THE POLAR BEAR – IT'S THE ONLY PLACE THEY SPAWN NATURALLY.

SURVIVAL ON THE Ice Plains is tough – it's a large biome where any water that is exposed is turned to ice and snow. You will find occasional Spruce trees, but they are rare, and there is a lower chance of mobs spawning here, although it does have it's own selection of hardy rabbits that like the cold! With food, wood and mobs scarce, it's a tough place to stay alive!

IF YOU'RE PLANNING TO GO MINING IN THE ICE PLAINS, YOU WILL FIND OAK TREES, SPRUCE TREES, SNOW, ICE AND THE ODD BIT OF TALL GRASS.

ICE PLAINS ARE RARE, BUT THERE'S AN EVEN RARER BIOME CALLED 'ICE PLAINS SPIKES' WHERE GIANT SPIKES OF PACKED ICE RISE INTO THE AIR UP TO 20 BLOCKS TALL!

BETTER TOGETHER

10 of the best multiplayer games in Minecraft

Minecraft can be a solitary experience. Sometimes we get caught up building cosy homes for ourselves. Other times, we spend hours and days underground, strip mining in the search for precious ore. You can spend so long on your lonesome you forget what other people's faces look like (boxy with square eyes, probably). But it doesn't have to be like that! There are loads of multiplayer options that change the game, offering fresh, exciting ways to play. But surely, Minecraft could never be that different, right? Wrong! You can experience thrilling prison breakouts, solve cunning puzzles, and even go racing.

Because servers can host many people at once, you can expect something totally different from your vanilla Minecraft experience. Some of the games on this list require you to join a server, others are maps you can download and play locally with friends. It's more than just PvP, too. If you're not in the mood for fighting, there are some great options here that prioritise co-operation over combat. We've also included details on how to join a multiplayer server in this feature. Over the next few pages you'll find 10 recommended maps, but don't stop there! There are loads to try, and even the simplest game can keep you entertained for weeks. You've been warned...

BLOCK PARTY
bit.ly/1WQ75SV

You may have seen a few prominent YouTubers playing this one, and it's easy to see why. It's brilliant – a funky dance-off that's the ultimate test of reactions and observation. Every few seconds a colour is selected and you have to seek it out. Soon other colours disappear, so if you don't groove your way to the necessary block in time, you're eliminated. As the game progresses, the time between each change gets shorter, so the game gets more frantic the longer you last. Throw in a few power-ups, and an in-game jukebox, and you have the sort of Minecraft game you can play indefinitely. To the dance floor with you!

IT'S BETTER TOGETHER
bit.ly/1tTKMub

The first clue is in the name. It's a cunning co-op map that recalls excellent puzzle game Portal 2. If you haven't played it – or even if you have, and you want to try something slightly different – this map is great. It's by FloddyFosh, creator of the Prince of Minecraftia map, but this time the 30+ puzzles all work with two players. You don't need any special mods or texture packs to play, either – just a friend and a keen mind. It's a great alternative to some of the more action-packed games on this list, but make sure you play it on Peaceful – it's hard to solve puzzles when they've been blown up by Creepers.

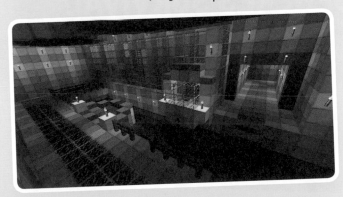

HOW TO PLAY ON A MULTIPLAYER SERVER

It's actually much easier than you'd think. All you need to do is connect to the IP address of a multiplayer server. Alternatively, you can download a multiplayer map and host the game yourself, by opening your home or local area network to other computers. If you're playing online, you and your friends can join together by selecting the same server. Simply log in to Minecraft, select Multiplayer and enter the IP or web address of the server you want.

However you choose to do it, all players must be running the same version of Minecraft. If this is a problem, you can tweak which version of the game you're running by making a new profile in the Minecraft launcher, then you can switch between profiles easily later on. Your other option is Minecraft Realms, Mojang's official multiplayer server service. It costs money to use, but there are loads of games to try, and you can set it up easily through the game client.

PRISONTECH 2.0
bit.ly/1iYliWS

You can't have a multiplayer map list without including a prison map, and this is one of the best. The server here is essentially a high security prison, and it's your job to escape. You earn money by selling stacks of goods, mined in gigantic pits beneath the prison. It sounds bleak, but it's actually great fun. As you work your way up, it becomes a PvP game, as other players try to steal your goods. What are you in prison for? It's best not to ask. I'm innocent, guv!

CASTLERISE: BROTHERS' FEUD
bit.ly/1XsZbPm

You only need to see the imposing stone structures to understand what this one's about. It's a team based PvP mini-game about siege warfare. Each team has a castle and a prince who they need to protect. You get a building phase, spending a set amount of money on your defences. Once that's done, you're given a basic set of armour, a sword, bow and arrows, and you have to break down your enemy's fortress. The first team to smash up the enemy's prince is the winner.

SPHERES SURVIVAL
bit.ly/24UFKOY

As well as looking pleasingly round, this is an excellent PvP map. A survival game for 2-4 players, you begin on a small sphere on which you gather resources for the coming conflict. Between you and the other players is a much larger sphere, packed with parkour trails, shadowy caves and loot. As you progress to the middle sphere, you'll inevitably bump into other players, creating flashpoints of random combat. It's a tricky one. When you die, you lose all your gear.

BLITZ SURVIVAL
bit.ly/1IZGCXP

This is another Hypixel one, and it's ace. It's a classic deathmatch that revolves around a special Blitz Star, which is released after five minutes. If you grab it, you'll get a random selection of powers. Once the game reaches the right number of players, a deathmatch countdown starts, throwing players into a small and deadly arena. The last player standing wins. It's a classic scenario with enough smart twists to make it stand out. You'll love it *puts on sunglasses* TO BLITZ.

HALF HEART RACE
bit.ly/1SxgKvQ

Half Heart Race is a little different. You'd probably already worked that out from the name. You have to manoeuvre your way through a whopping great parkour map, with a paltry two hearts (you only have the half-heart mentioned in the name if you're playing on the hardest setting). There are multiple routes through each map, each with their own risks and rewards. As you'd expect, there's no ability to regenerate hearts, so it's a cunning test of both speed and skill.

TURBO KART RACERS
bit.ly/2r0rg71

It's impossible to do a feature on multiplayer Minecraft games without talking about Hypixel – that's why they're on this list twice. Turbo Kart Racers is an ambitious kart racing game, with a staggering level of depth. We've rarely played a racing game with fewer features. There are loads of tracks to try, from weaving canyons to leafy jungles, as well as a collection of power-ups that puts Mario Kart to shame. Expect plasma shields, bombs, snowballs, swords squids and shells, in all the established Mario Kart colours.

DIVERSITY 2
bit.ly/1slsqRX

ARENA BRANCH

Here's an monument-style map that tasks you with completing a series of tasks, and it regularly comes high up on lists of the best Minecraft maps. Each monument block is obtained by completing a different kind of level, all of which can be played alone or with friends. It's a change from the more combative stuff on this list, and it'll really get your little grey cubes working. It looks great, too – a team of custom builders were enlisted to make it, and it features over 650 custom skins.

HUNGER GAMES
bit.ly/1DtUd6F

One of the most popular multiplayer Minecraft games, and it's not just because of the name. It's a fantastic PvP experience, a battle royale that combines survival, exploration and combat. You begin in the centre of a giant glass dome, and have to strike out, stock up and survive. You'll need to find a server hosting the map to play, which shouldn't be too hard, or you can download a map and host it yourself. Wasted49's map, which we've linked to above, is a good place to start.

KNOW YOUR BIOMES
#8 THE END

LURKING IN THE DARKNESS YOU CAN FIND THE END SHIP, USUALLY DOCKED NEAR A PIER IN THE END CITY. LOOKING VERY MUCH LIKE A PIRATE SHIP, IT'S WORTH TRYING TO GET ON BOARD USING AN ENDER PEARL AS THERE ARE RARE TREASURES TO BE HAD BELOW DECK IN THE TREASURE ROOM INCLUDING ELYTRA – WINGS THAT WILL LET YOU FLY!

IT'S NOT JUST BLACK WILDERNESS IN THE END, THIS BIOME ALSO GENERATES END CITIES ON ITS OUTER ISLANDS. TO GET HERE YOU MUST PASS THROUGH THE END PORTAL THAT APPEARS ONCE YOU HAVE DEFEATED THE ENDER DRAGON.

HOW GOOD ARE you at playing Minecraft? Have you made it to the third dimension yet – The End? To get here, you need to find, fix and activate the End Portal found in a Stronghold underground. It's where you will get to meet the Ender Dragon and armies of Endermen, so we hope you are brave enough! Although it's cold in The End, it never rains, it never snows, it's just black and packed with Shulkers!

STUFF FOUND IN THE END FOR YOUR COLLECTION OF LOOT INCLUDES END STONE, OBSIDIAN, END CRYSTALS, CHORUS PLANTS, END STONE BRICKS AND PURPUR BLOCKS.

SHULKERS SPAWN NATURALLY IN THE END CITIES AND DO NOT RESPAWN ONCE KILLED. AT NIGHT THE ENDERMEN WILL COME IN THEIR PACKS, IF YOU KILL ONE YOU MAY BE REWARDED WITH AN ENDER PEARL. THE ONLY OTHER MOB FOUND IN THE END IS THE ENDER DRAGON – AND THERE'S ONLY ONE OF THOSE!

THE ULTIMATE GUIDE TO THE END

Everything you need to know about reaching The End, fighting the Ender Dragon, and finding End Cities!

ALL ENDERMEN ARE NAMED GREGORY YOU KNOW!

Now that The End is in Pocket Edition and expanded on consoles there's suddenly a whole lot more exploring for you to do! The End can be a tricky, scary place, filled with annoying Endermen and lots of purple, but don't worry, we've put together a guide that covers everything. We'll show you how to make a portal to get there, how to beat the Ender Dragon, and how to find End Cities too. If you're lucky you might even find some Elytra to help you fly around!

1 ENDERMEN

Learning to fight these guys in the Overworld will help you in The End. They'll leave you alone if you don't look at them, but you'll need to fight them to get lots of Ender Pearls. They're fast and hard to fight, so make sure you have good armour and weapons. A good strategy is to make a 2 block high base, lure them nearby and then hit their legs. They're 3 blocks tall so can't get in.

2 ENDER PEARLS

You'll need lots of Ender Pearls to get to The End. You can get them by farming Endermen, but they also appear in some Chests in strongholds. You can also turn them into Eyes of Ender by adding Blaze Powder at a Crafting Table. If you make an Eye of Ender you can throw it and it'll help you find a stronghold with an End Portal in it.

3 END PORTAL

You can either make or find an End Portal. It's made of 3 End Portal Blocks on each side, and to activate it you have to put an Eye of Ender in all 12 blocks – each block facing the middle. If they face any other direction it won't work. You might have to stand in the middle to get the blocks the right way around.

> SHHH... I'M CREEPING UP ON STEVE!

ALWAYS BRING A BOW WITH YOU AS CREEPERS WILL EXPLODE IF THEY COME CLOSE TO YOU, BUT A BOW WILL KEEP THEM AWAY.

> WHAT? THERE'S A CREEPER BEHIND ME YOU SAY?!

4 PREPPING FOR BATTLE

There's a lot you need to do before you go through that portal! You can only leave if you beat the Ender Dragon or die, so you need to be well prepped before you venture out. You'll need a Diamond Sword, Pickaxe and Armour, as well as a Bow and plenty of Health Potions. A Pumpkin for your head will also help, and if you can, team up with friends and work together to beat it. It's much easier than fighting alone!

5 FIGHTING IN THE END

Fighting the Ender Dragon is just one part of The End, there are lots of other dangers to face while fighting! The End is filled with Endermen – so many that it's hard not to catch their attention. Wearing a Pumpkin Head can help, but it makes it hard to see the dragon. You might also spawn underground so you'll have to reach the surface first.

GREGORY ENDERMAN, AT YOUR SERVICE.

BOWS WILL BE NO USE HERE IN THE END, THE ENDERMEN WILL TELEPORT AWAY BEFORE YOUR ARROWS CAN POKE THEM!

6 ENDER CRYSTALS

Before you start fighting the Ender Dragon properly you'll want to destroy all of the Ender Crystals that heal it first. The best method is to shoot them with your Bow, but you'll have to climb the pillars of the ones protected by Iron Bars to destroy those before hitting the Crystal. If you destroy a Crystal while a dragon is charging from it you'll do a big chunk of damage at once.

7 KILLING THE DRAGON

B ecause it flies around, the Ender Dragon is really hard to hit. It's better to wait until it tries charging at you and then hit it in the head with a charged Arrow, then quickly dodge its attack. You might be able to get a second hit in when it recoils. Hitting its head does more damage than hitting its body.

WOW! THIS GUIDE TO THE END IS REALLY DRAGON ON!

8 GATEWAY PORTALS

A fter you kill the dragon a fountain will spawn in the middle that takes you back to the Overworld, but make sure you look around first! A Gateway Portal will also spawn, sometimes you'll find it in the sky. If you throw an Ender Pearl in it, it will teleport you to an Island in The End. You can spawn more Portals by beating the dragon again. Every time you beat it another Portal will spawn.

WHAT AM I DOING HERE? A NEW PLACE TO EXPLORE!

9 END CITIES

If you get lucky you might find an End City on the Island you teleport to through the Gateway Portal. They're full of Chests filled with enchanted weapons and other goodies, but also danger. Instead of stairs you might have to do some clever jumping to go up the floors in the City. You'll also have to look out for enemies.

10 SHULKERS

They might look like purple blocks with cute faces, but Shulkers can be really dangerous! They live in End Cities and shoot out projectiles that follow you around the room and make you levitate. You have to hit or block them to get rid of them – dodging doesn't work. They have really good defence so you need to hit them when they look out of their shells. They can drop Shulker Shells which can be used to make Shulker Boxes for storage.

ONCE YOU'VE KILLED A SHULKER BE SURE TO PICK UP ITS SHELL AS YOU CAN USE IT LIKE A BACKPACK AND EVEN COLOUR IT TO YOUR TASTE!

11 END SHIPS

These are ships that are sometimes found floating near **End Cities** if you're lucky. You'll have to build a bridge to reach one and once inside you'll have to beat the **Shulkers**, but it's worth it. Inside are at least 2 **Treasure Chests** and an **Item Frame** containing a pair of **Elytra** wings. They're super-rare to find though!

MAKE SURE YOU'VE GOT A GOOD COLLECTION OF ENDER PEARLS BEFORE YOU GET HERE – YOU CAN TELEPORT TO HARD TO REACH PLACES.

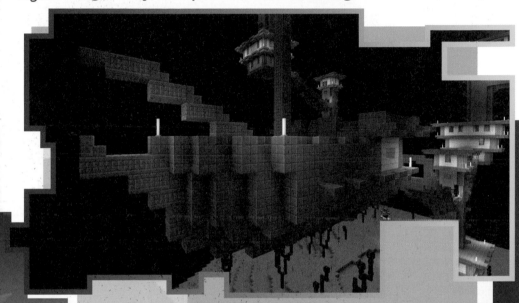

I CAN SEE MY HOUSE FROM UP HERE!

12 ELYTRA

The best item in the entire game! **Elytra** wings are placed in your **Chest Armour** slot and let you glide around the world. You activate them by hitting jump while falling and they'll let you glide around like a bird. They make getting around **The End** and the **Overworld** a lot more fun.

A-Z of MINECRAFT Tips

There are 1,000s of elements that make up the joy that is Minecraft, we could fill this book with things beginning with 'A' alone! We've put together an A-Z of the most essential hints, tips and facts...

A is for...
ARMOUR

PROTECT YOURSELF from damage with a combo of boots, leggings, chest plates and helmets. The player can use armour, but some mobs can too to protect themselves from your attacks!

B is for...
BLOCKS

THE BASIC building 'blocks' that all Minecraft worlds are created from. They can be solids or liquids, and all are able to be mined then used in your own creations. Most blocks are not affected by gravity.

C is for...
CRAFTING

MATERIALS, BLOCKS and tools can be created by crafting them from items. There's a basic 2x2 crafting grid in your inventory, for more complex recipes that need a 3x3 grid you will have to make or find a Crafting Table.

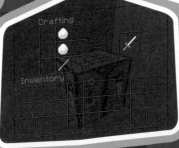

D is for...
DRAGON

ENDER DRAGON to be precise. This giant beast is found in The End. You must kill it with skilled use of the bow and arrow then sword when it gets close enough, but first destroy the Ender Crystals found here!

E is for...
END PORTAL

IT'S THROUGH the End Portal that you travel to The End. You must find a naturally occurring one in Survival mode, but in Creative you can just make your own by placing End Portal Frames then filling them with Eyes Of Ender.

F is for...
FOOD

YOU'VE GOT to eat, or you will starve to death! Luckily, most food items can be stacked in your inventory so you can stock up well before an adventure. Eating improves your hunger bar, shown with hearts.

G is for...
GLOWSTONE

THESE ARE only found in The Nether and shine at the brightest level. As well being handy as a light, they are useful in Redstone circuits where they transmit the signal through the block to nearby Redstone.

H is for...
HORSE

THERE ARE five kinds of horse: regular horses, mules, donkeys, skeleton horses and zombie horses. They are all tameable mobs, by placing a saddle and jumping on you can control which direction it walks.

I is for...
IRON GOLEM

THESE GIANTS hit harder than nearly any other mob – the Iron Golem is the protector of Villagers and will be out to get you if you mess with them! They love Villagers so much, they give them bunches of flowers.

L is for...
LLAMA

WHILE THEY might spit if you hit them, Llamas are great mobs that can be tamed and used to carry around all of your heavy stuff! You can't ride and control a Llama, but you can put a lead on one and guide it along.

J is for...
JUKEBOX

GOT A stack of Music Discs and don't know how to play them? You need a Jukebox! They can be Crafted using 8 Wood Planks and a Diamond. With a Music Disc in your hand, Right-click on the Jukebox to play it.

K is for...
KNOCKBACK

WHEN GOING in for an attack you've got to be careful of Knockback! This is the measure of how many blocks both you, and your enemy, will be knocked back by each attack. Be especially careful around cliff edges!

Iron Sword (#0267)
Knockback II
When in main hand:
1.6 Attack Speed
6 Attack Damage
minecraft:iron_sword
NBT: 1 tag(s)

M is for...
MOBS
WE'RE ALWAYS going on about Mobs – these are the 'mobile' characters in the game. Each biome has different mobs that spawn, some will have babies and some must be made or spawned with eggs.

N is for...
NETHER PORTAL
TO TRAVEL between the Overworld and the Nether you have to go through a Nether Portal. The frame must be made from Obsidian, at least 4x5 in dimension, then lit with any fire source to open the Portal.

O is for...
OBSERVER
THIS IS a special block (with a face on it) that will 'observe' other blocks for changes and give out a Redstone signal. Useful for monitoring things like crops growing, weather changing and lots of other cool stuff.

P is for...
PARROTS
PARROTS ARE brilliant! They spawn in Jungles and come in five colours. These lovely birds won't attack you, you can tame them by feeding them seeds – they will even sit on your shoulder so you can be a pirate!

S is for...
SHULKER
FOUND ON the outer islands of The End, Shulkers look just like regular Purpur at first, but when you get close they will crack open and the Shulker inside will fire a bullet at you that will follow you around until it hits!

Q is for...
QUARTZ
CRAFTERS USE Quartz to give their buildings the look of marble. It's a decorative block that can be Crafted from Nether Quartz, only found in The Nether, and itself only made from Nether Quartz Ore and a fuel like Wood.

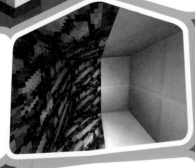

R is for...
REDSTONE
THE ELECTRICITY of Minecraft. The flat blocks are see-through and will carry the power of Redstone. Placing it on the ground as Redstone Dust, you can make power circuits for your inventions.

T is for...
TNT

CRAFTED FROM Gunpowder and Sand, a TNT block will give you an explosion. Want a bigger bang? Just pile a few on top of each other. They also appear naturally in Desert Temples and Woodland Mansions. BANG!

U is for...
UNDEAD

SOME MOBS are 'undead'. Skeletons, the Wither, Zombies, Husk, Zombie Pigman, Zombie Horse and Skeleton Horse. Use a Potion of Harm on them, they will heal! Use a Potion of Healing, they'll be harmed!

V is for...
VEX

WHEN A bunch of Evokers get together in battle, they will summon a Vex attack. You'll know when a Vex is coming as there will be white smoke and a horn will sound! The Vex is a ghost-like mob with a sword!

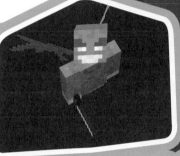

W is for...
WITHER

A SUPER scary boss mob, the Wither can be spawned by making a T-shape of Soul Sand blocks and placing 3 Wither Skeleton Skulls on top. It has three heads and will spit out skulls in all directions then explode!

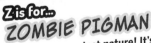

Z is for...
ZOMBIE PIGMAN

IT'S A crime against nature! It's not a Zombie, it's not a Pig – it's a Zombie Pigman! These mobs spawn in The Nether, out of Nether Portals or can appear just from Pigs if they are struck by lightning!

X is for...
XMAS CHEST

PLAY BETWEEN Christmas Eve and Boxing Day and you will find that all the Chests have changed into special Xmas Chests that look like presents. Here's a secret: change the date on your computer to see them!

Y is for...
YELLOW WOOL

OK, THERE are lots of things that are yellow. Wool actually comes in 16 colours and can be broken using any tool in the game, but a pair of Shears are the most effective tool to use. Where can you find wool? On a Sheep!

WHICH MOB ARE YOU?

START

Have you ever left the Overworld?

- **N** → **Do you like to explore?**
- **Y** → **Are you prone to fits of hissing?**

Do you like to explore?
- **Y** → **Do you wander around aimlessly?**
- **N** → **Do you feel uneasy around omelettes?**

Are you prone to fits of hissing?
- **Y** → **Are you slightly undead?**
- **N** → **Do you like to ride around on spiders?**

Do you wander around aimlessly?
- **Y** → **Are you immune to damage when you fall?**
- **N** → Cluck, cluck, cluck?

Do you feel uneasy around omelettes?
- **Y** → **Are you immune to damage when you fall?**
- **N** → **Do you like Steve?**

Are you slightly undead?
- **N** → **Do you like Steve?**
- **Y** → **Are you happiest in the sunshine?**

Do you like to ride around on spiders?
- **N** → **Are you happiest in the sunshine?**
- **Y** → Do you have a bow and arrow?

Are you immune to damage when you fall?
- **N** → Cluck, cluck, cluck?
- **Y** → Ever been chased by an Ocelot?

Do you like Steve?
- **N** → Are you likely to suddenly explode?
- **Y** → **Are you happiest in the sunshine?**

Are you happiest in the sunshine?
- **N** → Are you likely to suddenly explode?

Cluck, cluck, cluck? — Cluck! → Ever been chased by an Ocelot?
- **Eh?** → VILLAGER

Ever been chased by an Ocelot?
- **Y** → CHICKEN
- **N** → VILLAGER

Are you likely to suddenly explode?
- **Y** → CREEPER
- **N** → Do you have a bow and arrow?

Do you have a bow and arrow?
- **Y** → SKELETON
- **N** → CREEPER

VILLAGER

You are a smart, inventive, honest kind of soul, who likes nothing more than hard work and exploring your surroundings.

CHICKEN

Life is best for you when you have no plan, and you like to wander about randomly. Kind, friendly, and great for dinner.

CREEPER

You have a habit of popping up when no one expects you, mostly when it's getting dark. You're also noted for your explosive temper.

SKELETON

Much misunderstood, you have a love of archery and riding. But if anybody gets on your wrong side it could end badly.

PAGE 14
GUESS THE MOB
1 = Enderman, 2 = Skeleton, 3 = Villager, 4 = Zombie, 5 = Witch

PAGE 25
WEAPON SUDOKU

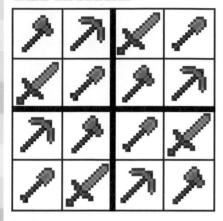

PAGE 25
NAME THAT BLOCK
1 = Grass, 2 = Netherrack, 3 = Gold Ore, 4 = Magma, 5 = Redstone, 6 = Slime, 7 = TNT

PAGE 25
HOW MANY SPIDERS?
There were 10!

PAGE 58
SPOT THE DIFFERENCE

PAGE 73
CREEPER SEARCH

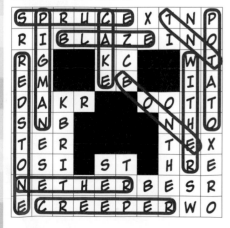

PAGE 16-21
THE ULTIMATE MINECRAFT QUIZ

1. What is the minimum amount of blocks needed to make a Nether Portal?
A. 10

2. Which biome do Ocelots spawn in?
B. Jungle

3. How long is a day in Minecraft?
C. 20 minutes

4. What potion effect do you get when you use a Rabbit's Foot in brewing?
A. Leaping

5. If a Villager gets struck by lightning, what happens to them?
C. They turn into a witch

6. Name the man who created Minecraft and sold it for $3.5 billion!
C. Notch

7. Which of these are multiplayer games in console Minecraft...
A. Tumble
C. Glide

8. How do you craft a bed?
A. 3 Wool and 3 Wood Planks

9. Which is the rarest Ore?
C. Emerald

10. What happens when a Creeper gets struck by lightning?
A. It turns into a super-charged Creeper with larger blast radius

11. What type of tools run out the quickest?
B. Golden tools

12. Name the dragon found in The End.
A. The Ender Dragon

13. What happens if you eat Chorus Fruit found in The End?
B. You are teleported to a location within 8 blocks

14. What is the name of the story game created by Telltale Games?
B. Minecraft: Story Mode

15. Which items do you need to bake a cake?
C. 1 Egg, 2 Sugar, 3 Wheat, 3 Milk Buckets

16. Which substance acts as electricity in Minecraft?
C. Redstone

17. How do you get saddles?
B. They are found in spawned buildings

18. Which country was Minecraft originally made in?
B. Sweden

19. How many different kinds of biomes are there in PC Minecraft? (Two are unused!)
A. 63

20. What do pigs eat?
C. Carrots

21. What do you use to mine stone with?
B. Pickaxe

22. Which of these items do Zombies NOT drop...
C. Candy Floss

23. Which of these blocks cannot be pushed by a Piston?
A. Melon Block

24. How many types of tree are there in Minecraft?
C. 6

25. What kind of Ore is found in The Nether?
C. Nether Quartz

26. Which of these is NOT a Minecraft mob?
B. Crocodile

27. How many colours of Wool are there?
A. 16

28. What do Squid drop when killed?
B. Ink Sacs

29. How many hearts of damage does an ordinary Diamond Sword deal?
B. 7 Hearts

30. How do you tame Wolves?
A. Give them a bone

PAGE 48-51
31. Which piece of armour protects you the most?
C. Chestplate

32. How many types of Horse Armour are there?
C. 4

33. Which of these is NOT a Minecraft block?
C. Marshmallow

34. What happens when you try to shoot an Enderman?
B. The Enderman teleports away before the arrow hits them

35. Which of these is NOT a food in Minecraft?
C. Vegetable Stew

36. What happens when you eat a Pufferfish?
A. You get poisoned for a few seconds

37. What happens when you walk on Soul Sand?
A. You walk much slower than normal

38. What is the default female skin called in Minecraft?
B. Alex

39. What happens when you hit a Llama?
C. It spits at you

40. What happens when you name a mob 'Dinnerbone'?
B. It will turn upside-down

41. How were Creepers invented?
A. Notch made a mistake while making Pigs

42. What tool do you use for farming?
C. Hoe

43. What is the default male skin called in Minecraft?
A. Steve

44. What year was Minecraft officially released to the public?
B. 2011

45. What type of tool must you mine Obsidian with?
C. Diamond Pickaxe

46. What happens when a Pig is struck by lightning?
C. It turns into a Zombie Pigman

47. What is the name of the naturally spawning mob that lives in villages?
A. Villager

48. Which mob is found inside an End City?
C. Shulker

49. What is the name of the mob that is summoned with 2 Snow Blocks and 1 Pumpkin?
B. Snow Golem

50. What block can be crafted with Sand and Gunpowder?
C. TNT